All About Cats

TS

⊃J

⊃J

TS

All About Cats

Joan Palmer

WARD LOCK LIMITED·LONDON

F

Acknowledgments
The author would like to thank Pedigree Petfoods
Education Centre for their help and encouragement; Mrs
Grace Pond, FZS, organizer of the National Cat Club
Show, for suggesting my invaluable visit; Mrs Kay
Burgess, Chairman of the Surrey and Sussex Cat
Association, for the honour of judging non-pedigrees at
their Championship Show, and Miss Kathy Taylor (Saxon
Siamese), for proving how helpful a steward should be.
Finally, grateful thanks are due to my husband, Doug, a
lifelong 'ailurophile', and Samson, our Siamese cat, who
knew it all.

Joan Palmer

The author and publishers would also like to thank the
following for supplying extra pictures for the book: Sally
Ann Thompson/Animal Photography Ltd pages 66, 74
and 90; Reg Wilson page 14.

Previous page: The tabby moggy is a
familiar sight in the homes and
gardens of Britain.

Illustrations © Ward Lock and Uitgeverij Het Spectrum B. V.
De Meern, The Netherlands 1980, 1986.

Text © Ward Lock Limited 1986.

First published in Great Britain in 1986
by Ward Lock Limited, 8 Clifford Street,
London WIX IRB, an Egmont Company.

Designed by Heather Sherratt
Text filmset in 11 point Palatino
by Preface Ltd., Salisbury, Wilts

Printed and bound in Czechoslovakia

British Library Cataloguing in Publication Data

Palmer, Joan
 All about cats.
 1. Cats—Juvenile literature
 I. Title
 636.8   SF445.7

 ISBN 0-7063-6297-7

Contents

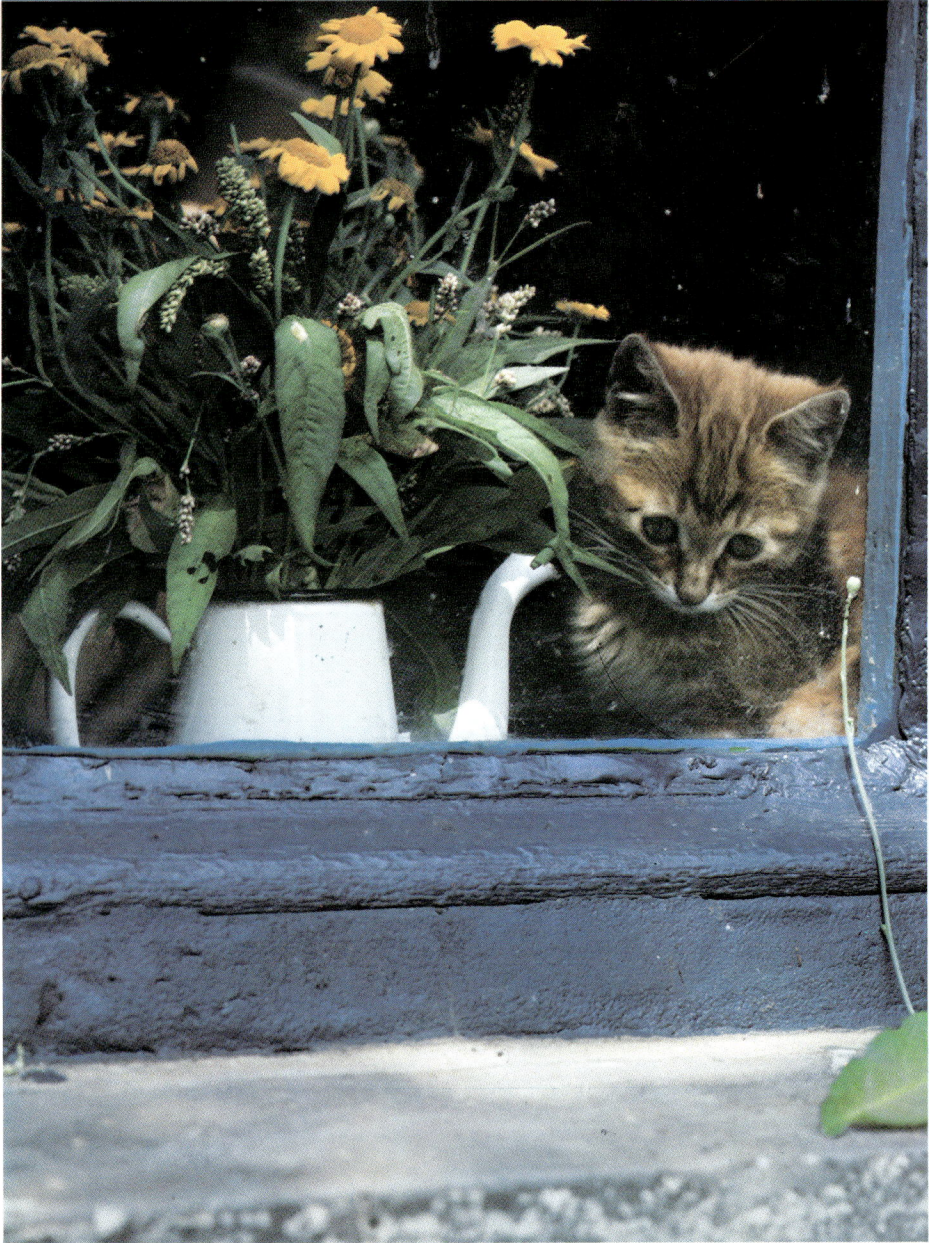

The history of the cat

There are millions of cats; more than four and a half million in Britain alone, ranging from those whose parents, and grandparents, are prize-winners, to the familiar tabby or ginger tom we see snoozing by the fireside.

The cat evokes strong emotions. You love cats, or hate them, are allergic to their fur, and scared of their inscrutable stare; or offer them slavish devotion to which, after all, they are due; for in common with the Imperial Pekingese, our ancient friend, the cat, has to come to terms with a less revered life in the western hemisphere.

Cats, wild and tame

The history of the cat can be traced back millions of years, to a small weasel-like creature, the miacis, which was the forerunner of many animals, including dogs, hyenas, bears and civets. It was from the civets that the *Felidae* or felines (cat family) evolved.

The cat still closely resembles, and shares many characteristics with the larger members of the feline race; the lions, tigers, leopards and cheetahs, which one sees in the zoo. It has the same rough tongue, and razor-sharp teeth and, because it walks on its toes, it is able to stalk its prey stealthily. In common with the big cats, it has retractable claws and a long, supple body; its paws are cushioned with pads for quiet stalking and, with the exclusion of the Manx cat variety, its long tail is an aid to balance.

Little is known about the very first domestic or pet cats. It is thought that by living close to, and being fed by humans, the smaller wild cats, probably the Caffre-Kaffir of Africa gradually became tame. Possibly they mated with other smaller, wild cats, becoming the ancestors of the pet cats we have today. The Kaffir cat still looks very like one of the modern varieties, the Abyssinian.

Man's friend

From paintings on the walls of tombs, statues, and mummified cats found in little wooden coffins, we can be sure that cats were treasured by the Ancient Egyptians more than four thousand years ago. They became the guardians of the granaries by keeping down

Left: The appealing gaze of the kitten helps to make the cat one of Britain's most popular pets.

The feline family includes not only the domestic cat, but much larger members too, like this leopard.

rats and mice, and their hunting instincts were put to the test in catching wild fowl for their masters. Over 1,000 years ago, cats were known in China, and later in Japan where they were used to keep the mice away from the silkworm cocoons and valuable manuscripts.

It was the Egyptians who noticed that the pupils of a cat's eyes altered according to the light; and that cats always had large numbers of kittens. They began to think there must be something magical about them, so they were worshipped as gods, even the poorest homes keeping a cat. To kill one would ensure severe punishment.

The Egyptians worshipped a number of gods and goddesses, many being shaped like humans, but having animal heads. The cat was thought to be sacred to the Egyptian goddess Isis. Gradually it became recognized as an incarnation of deity and it was as the daughter of Isis, and her husband, Osiris, the sun god, that the cat goddess Bast (Bastet or Pasht) emerged. It is from 'Pasht' that the pet name, puss, was derived.

Bast was generally represented by a cat's head on a human body. However, when the numerous Egyptian gods came into being, the cat was revered for its qualities of ferocity and its prowess as huntress, so that the original statues were constructed lion-headed, and although Bast later came to be known as a cat-headed goddess, she never ceased to be worshipped as a lion-headed deity, statues in both forms co-existing during the last thousand years of paganism.

In the twenty-second dynasty (about 950 BC) Bast took precedence over all other goddesses, becoming known as the Lady of Bubastis.

On an island in the Nile, a large statue in the likeness of Bast, was erected in the temple of Bubastis to which thousands would travel, by boat, on feast days, so that they might worship.

King Osorkon II, of Egypt, built a magnificent hall in Bubastis

Below: As this British Red Short-hair stealthily stalks its prey, we are reminded of the domestic cats close connections to the larger member of the feline race, such as the tiger, lion and leopard.

which he dedicated to the goddess, and a relief, found on the walls, proclaims his allegiance thus: 'I give thee every land in obeisance, I give thee all power like Ra' (the sun god).

When cats died, their bodies were mummified and the richer the family of their owners, the more ornate and valuable the coffins would be. Some which have been discovered even contained little mummified mice so that the cats would not hunger on their last journey. Mourning for the cats was real and intense, the bereaved family shaving off their eyebrows to express their grief. And, of course, living cats were zealously guarded; they were not officially allowed out of Egypt though a few did find their way to other parts of the world.

It is thought that the first domestic cat came to Britain in the first or second century AD, brought by the invading Romans, a belief verified by footprints in clay tiles, and bones discovered in the remains of Roman villas.

And, by the tenth century, the Welsh Prince Howel the Wise fixed the price of a new-born kitten at one penny – worth very much more in those days – the price being increased when the ability of the kitten to catch mice had been proved.

Sadly, in the Middle Ages, in Britain, and other parts of the world, cats became feared and even hated, because they were thought to be unlucky (black cats especially) and to be connected with black magic. Poor old men and women were thought to be wizards and witches simply because they owned a pet cat.

One wonders, however, at the gullibility of those who, in 1566, obtained a confession from sixty-four-year-old Agnes Waterhouse of Hatfield Peverell, Essex, whom they later hanged for witchcraft. The confession stated that she had despatched her black cat 'Satan' to spoil butter, kill a neighbour's stock and 'bewitch' a man to death. Today if a black cat should chance to cross our path, we believe we are in for a spell of *good* luck!

The witches were supposed to be able to change themselves into cats, or to ride on broomsticks with their cat familiars as their passengers. Cat owners were reckoned to be in league with the Devil and many innocent people were tried and put to death with their pets. A witch hunt had also become a cat hunt, despite the fact that the cat had proved itself by now as an ally of man in his fight against the rat, the common enemy which had led to the Black Death, or Bubonic Plague, which spread into Europe from Asia in the thirteenth century and eventually wiped out half of London in 1666. Not until the eighteenth century was it realized that the cat was not only an excellent companion but a formidable opponent of the brown rat which invaded warehouses where foodstuffs were stored. The cat became known, probably because it disposed of the 'dirty rat', as being essentially a clean animal which might be allowed, and seen, in food shops without fear of disease or contamination.

Slowly, but surely, the cat became recognized as an ideal pet for the old and lonely. Poets, artists and writers began to write about them, and artists began to paint their special favourites; so that by the time Queen Victoria ascended the throne, most houses, shops and farms kept cats as mousers or as pets.

Right: The Abyssinian is thought to be very close in outline to the Ancient Egyptian cat.

But, forgetting for a moment the cat's prowess as a destroyer of vermin, its beauty, grace and the care the queen (female cat) lavished on her kittens, seemed, to the Victorians, to represent the most desirable traits of family life; and illustrations abounded of mother cats, with their families, while homes boasted cushions and samplers embroidered with cat designs; porcelain and china cats graced the mantelpiece, and chocolate boxes were adorned with pretty, feline pictures. The most famous cat illustrator of the period was Louis William Wain (1860–1939), whose picture postcard series of cats portraying nursery rhyme characters have now become collectors' items.

The cat had also become a sought-after pantomine figure, in performances of *Puss in Boots* and *Dick Whittington and his Cat* staged at Drury Lane and other big London theatres.

Puss in Boots was the invention of a French poet and critic, Charles Perrault, and was included in a collection of his fairy stories. Later it was translated into English by Robert Samber, and published, in Britain in 1729, under the title *Mother Goose's Tales*. Although 'Puss' wears boots and talks like a human being, his audacity and cunning are essentially cat characteristics.

Puss in Boots and his beautiful ladylove the White Cat appear in Tchaikovsky's ballet *The Sleeping Beauty*, first performed in 1890 in St. Petersburg (now Leningrad), Russia. The White Cat enters in the procession of wedding guests, carried on a cushion and serenely washing her face in the midst of all the grand company. Puss in Boots courts her in a delightful dance, accompanied by an oboe, which imitates the cats' mewing. This ballet is based on the story by Charles Perrault.

The tale of Dick Whittington and his cat is not, likewise, a fairy story, but based on the real-life history of Richard Whittington (*circa* 1358–1423), the third son of Sir William Whittington of Pauntley, Gloucester.

Whittington was apprenticed, in about 1371, to a member of the Mercer's Company in London, probably, in fact, the pantomime character, Sir John Fitzwarren, whose daughter Alice he married. Dick Whittington was a great philanthropist who enjoyed enormous wealth and prestige, and did indeed become Lord Mayor of London on no less than four occasions.

The only doubts about the authenticity of the Whittington pantomime centre around Dick's famous cat companion, and the picture of Dick as a poor boy, seeking his fortune in the cheerless streets of London seeing if they were really made of gold.

These facts do not seem likely when mindful of Dick's aristocratic birth. However, the cat may not be legendary, for the Reverend Samuel Lyons, an accredited biographer of Whittington, writes of a fifteenth-century figure of a boy with a cat discovered at a house in Gloucester once occupied by the Whittington family; and according to the historian, William Maitland, when the Newgate Prison was rebuilt following the Great Fire of London, there was found, midst the ruins, a figure of a boy with the word 'Libertas' carved on his hat, and a companion at his feet.

One can to this day visit the Whittington Stone at Holloway, north London, where Dick, in despair, sat pondering when the Bow

Left: A black, short-haired cat. Such pets were once thought to be the instruments of Satan, the 'familiars' of witches. Nowadays it is thought lucky if one crosses our path.

Bells rang out, urging him: 'Turn again, Whittington, Lord Mayor of London.' And, on nearby Highgate Hill, is the statue of Dick's cat, posed looking over its shoulder as if it too were listening to the prediction of its beloved master's future.

Cats in legend and literature

The first verses a child utters may be those concerning our friend, the cat:

'I love little pussy, her coat is so warm,
And if I don't hurt her, she'll do me no harm.'

'Pussy-cat, pussy-cat, where have you been?
I've been to London to see the Queen.
Pussy-cat, pussy-cat, what did you there?
I frightened a little mouse under her chair.'

We must not forget 'Hey diddle diddle, the cat and the fiddle, The cow jumped over the moon'; and, of course, 'Ding, dong, bell, Pussy's in the well'; and 'Three little kittens they lost their mittens'.

In later years, the child is introduced to Lewis Carroll's *Alice in Wonderland* becoming acquainted with the Cheshire cat who, on hearing the command, 'Off with his head' has the ability to vanish at will, barring its grin. 'This time it vanished,' wrote Carroll, 'beginning with the end of the tail and ending with the grin.' Actually, the famous Cheshire cheeses were once marked with the face of a cat and the saying 'to grin like a Cheshire cat' was in use long before Lewis Carroll put pen to paper. The saying may derive from the open-mouthed wolf heads on the arms of the eleventh century Earl of Chester and not from the Cheshire cat at all. Still, who, even in adulthood, could forget the argument put forth by the cat in '*Alice*' to confirm its insanity? 'Unlike the dog,' it said, 'who growls when it is angry and wags its tail when it is pleased, I growl when I am pleased and wag my tail when I am angry.'

But next come Edward Lear's wonderful nonsense poems, like 'The Owl and the Pussy-cat'.

Beatrix Potter's *The Tale of Tom Kitten*; and the cats which appear in Aesop's fables, mostly as the villains of the piece.

Older children enjoy *Old Possum's Book of Practical Cats* with T. S. Eliot's amusing verses about cats with such splendid names as Mungo-Jerrie and Rumpelteazer; Macavity, the ginger cat who was a master criminal, and the perverse, capricious Rum Tum Tugger.

On then to the classics, and our scholar will find that Swinburne, Wordsworth and Tennyson all wrote poems about cats; and that the American, Mark Twain, author of *Huckleberry Finn*, declared that 'A home without a cat, and a well-fed, well-petted and properly revered cat, may be a perfect home, perhaps, but how can it prove its title?'

In Rudyard Kipling's *Just So* stories we find 'The Cat that Walked by Himself'. There is also the sad tale of Selima, written by Thomas Gray, 'Ode on the death of a favourite cat drowned in a tub of gold fishes', in verses as elegant as the lamented cat herself.

More recently, Paul Gallico's book *Jennie*, Doreen Tovey's *Cats in*

Left: Puss in Boots and the White Cat in the Royal Ballet's production of Tchaikovsky's ballet *The Sleeping Beauty*. Here they dance before the wedding festivities begin.

the Belfry, and Derek Tangye's *A Cat at the Window* have proved very popular with both young and old.

And a study of the works of the great masters will also reveal cats, for they have been included in paintings by Leonardo da Vinci, Dürer, Hogarth, the Swiss painter Mind, Reynolds, Toulouse-Lautrec and, more recently, Picasso.

Despite the cat's association with the Devil, which I will shortly touch on, it has also been much favoured by men of God. Indeed, the prophet, Mohammed was a cat lover and the story has often been told of how, when his pet cat Muezza fell asleep in the sleeve of his garment, he had the sleeve cut off rather than disturb his feline friend.

The dog, apart from the fleet-footed Saluki, is, in Arab countries, an outcast of Allah; but the cat, beloved of the prophet, is to this day treated kindly by Moslems and is allowed access into a mosque.

Pope Gregory I had a pet cat, as did Pope Gregory III; and Cardinal Wolsey owned a cat, which was his constant companion and accompanied him to many religious meetings and services. Cardinal Richelieu of France also loved cats and particularly liked to have kittens around him.

There was also a welcome for puss in many an austere monastery where he became friend and dispeller of vermin. There is on record a verse written long ago by an Irish monk, about a cat with the unlikely name of Pangur Ban; the modern translation, by Robin Flower, would be:

'I and Pangur Ban, my cat,
'Tis a like task we are at;
Hunting mice is his delight,
Hunting words I sit all night.'

But still it is with the mysterious, the supernatural, that cats have been linked for centuries.

It was thought in particular that the Black Cat, a creature of darkness, who moved with stealth and had gleaming green eyes, must be in league, with the Devil. And when the Order of Knights Templar was quashed by Pope Clement V in the fourteenth century, its members admitted, under torture, that they were indeed Devil worshippers and had worshipped their deity in the form of a black tom cat. Doubtless the pain inflicted would have caused the victims to admit to anything, but thereafter cat lovers were viewed with suspicion.

Mythologically the suspicion is sound because the Egyptian cat goddess, Bast, was linked with Diana the moon goddess, or goddess of darkness, who later was to become Hecate, the Queen of all the Witches. Now Diana had a brother Lucifer, a god of light, whom she greatly desired, but who did not return her affections, choosing instead to sleep with a beautiful white cat. One night Diana persuaded the cat to change places with her, lay with Lucifer and bore, from the union, a daughter Aradia. She was later sent to earth by Diana to teach humans the art of witchcraft and, indeed, the beginnings of black magic, all because Diana had changed places with a beautiful white fairy cat.

Right: A beautiful seal-point Siamese. This type was introduced into Britain in 1884 and is still the best known of pedigree cats. The breed does not deserve its reputation for destructiveness, but it can be noisy and demanding.

Sailors, particularly, lay great store by a cat's supernatural powers and the word 'cat' enters many nautical expressions. A cat's paw is a light breeze, a cat-boat, a single masted vessel, a cat-head the beam for carrying the anchor; the cat-boat's rigging is known as the cat-rig and the act of hanging the anchor on the cat-head is talked about as 'catting the anchor'. The Slavs believe that, during thunderstorms, the bodies of cats are taken over by devils; and in Scotland when a cat indulges itself in scratching the furniture it is said to be raising the wind.

Cats have always been credited with the ability not only to foretell, but change the weather at will; and in Ireland, storm-raising cats would be gathered and held down until, in bad weather, they used their magic powers to bring about a calm. They are animals which seem throughout time to have been feared and revered. Happily, cats are treasured as much by people today as they were in the days of the Ancient Egyptians.

The Cat Fancy

It was in 1871, with cat popularity rising, that a Mr Harrison Weir had the great idea of running a cat show, so that people might see how beautiful cats could be. Thousands queued up to see them in the Crystal Palace, the magnificent exhibition centre in south London, later to be tragically destroyed by fire. And, thereafter, people began the selective breeding of cats, many of the famous, including Queen Victoria, owning unusual types.

It was rare in those days to know the names of a cat's parents and grandparents. But it was soon discovered that, by mating cats of the same colour, or coat patterns, kittens could be produced resembling the tom cat and queen. Careful records were written out, giving details of each cat used for breeding, and before long pedigree certificates were being issued, and it was possible to trace back to a cat's great-great-grandparents.

As more cat shows were held, visitors came from all over the world to admire the beautiful cats in Britain. Many bought prizewinners which they took back to their homelands. The USA started to hold cat shows and soon cats were just as popular there. Today there are shows in many other parts of the world, but the largest is held in Britain, with over 2,000 cats appearing in the National Cat Club Show at Olympia, west London.

The National Cat Club was established in 1887 with the aim of promoting the breeding of pure-bred cats and the running of cat shows. But in 1898, Lady Marcus Beresford formed a rival organization, The Cat Club, the aims of which were identical. For seven years The Cat Club bravely struggled on. It did not measure up to the task and The National Cat Club again reigned supreme. But there was more competition to come in the form of another newly formed group, this time calling themselves The Cat Fanciers' Association, until, in 1910 following much squabbling between 'ailurophiles' (devotees of the domestic cat), a conference of interested parties was called at which agreement to form The Governing Council of The Cat Fancy was reached.

The first General Meeting of this august body was held at the Inns of Courts Hotel, London, on 11 October, 1910. Seventy years later it is still the powerful Governing Council of The Cat Fancy which provides for the registration of cats and cat pedigrees, classifies cat breeds, approves cat shows, and does all within its power to improve cat breeding and welfare.

The council has a large number of affiliated Cat Clubs, all of which may, when their membership totals one hundred persons, appoint a delegate to the council. They may appoint two delegates if membership reaches 150, but should it fall below the required figure, the club loses its right to representation. However, some historic, specialist clubs, like the Siamese Cat Club are allowed representation irrespective of membership level.

Over the past few years, cats have again enjoyed a rise in popularity. The pundits say it is because they are a 'convenient' pet. But I wonder!

True the cat may be an easier animal to keep than a dog – after all, you don't have to take it for walks! But does anyone really own, or keep a pet cat? The cat decides whether it wishes to live with us. It enjoys an independence of life and spirit that most of us wish we could emulate, and we are enriched by its presence in our home.

Domesticated and working cats

Most domestic cats live out their lives as companions, and what better occupation could there be? There are, however, those who 'earn' their living, have their name on a pay-roll, or command high fees.

For instance, Peta (a female Manx) is the latest, and possibly the last of the line, in a succession of Home Office cats who were always called Peter.

On the death of her predecessor, the Governor of the Isle of Man offered to present the Home Office with a replacement. Peta was born on 1 October 1963, and presented to the Home Secretary of the time, the Right Hon. Henry Brooke, on 8 May 1964. Her appointment was greeted with great interest, particularly in America, where her story has appeared in several publications.

Peta is still alive, although getting on in years. Her official station is the Home Office, Main Building, at 50 Queen Anne's Gate, London, but she is at present enjoying semi-retirement at her country home where she has the benefit of a large garden belonging to a member of staff. She has a Treasury allowance of £13 per annum.

There has been a Peter the Cat at the Home Office since the 1800s, but in 1929 the Treasury made the cat official by granting 1d. a day for its food. This was adjusted from time to time so that Peta's predecessor, Peter, had a grant of £6. 10s. 0d. per annum. He was born in 1949 and served as the Home Office official cat for some sixteen years until his death on 9 March 1964. He is buried at the PDSA (People's Dispensary for Sick Animals) sanatorium at Ilford in Essex. Peter wore a tartan collar from which hung a medallion bearing his name. He appeared several times on television programmes and once on radio, and graced the front of the Home Office Sports Association Christmas cards in 1958, an honour bestowed on him after his tenth year of faithful service.

Sadly, times change, and with the rather larger office blocks now occupied by the Home Office, it is thought that these do not really provide a suitable home for a cat. Peta (pedigree name Manninagh Katedhu) will probably be the last of the line!

Mind you, there are other cats at Government level for, not so long ago, the RSPCA (Royal Society for the Prevention of Cruelty to Animals) received a request, from 10 Downing Street, to provide a cat to get rid of invading mice. Thereafter, the police were expected to ring the door bell at any time should Wilberforce, the mighty mouser, wish to get in . . . or out!

The Post Office has also employed cats on its staff. But since the demise of their famed Blacky at St Martin's-le-Grand, there are now only two London cats on the official pay-roll. These moggies receive £1 a week for food in return for mousing duties and defend the mail in the sorting offices at North Western District Office and Bethnal Green.

The British Museum in London is not only the last resting place of several mummified, cat-worshipping, Ancient Egyptians, and one mummified sacred cat; it is also said to provide food and shelter for seven cats in return for mousing duties around its less frequented apartments. Their existence is well-ordered – signs posted in the nether corridors indicate the 'authorised cat feeding place' and other areas where it is 'strictly forbidden to feed cats'. *The New Yorker* magazine recently recorded the existence of a British Museum Cats'

The domestic cat offers companionship for the old and lonely; but not all cats lead such a leisurely life. Many have to 'earn' their living as mousers or advertising models.

21

Welfare Society, which ensures that life is not unpleasant for the chosen seven. That number of cats is permitted by order of the Director's Office; perhaps inspired by the seven cats in the old rhyme 'As I was going to St. Ives'.

Once upon a time bakeries were plagued with mice and bakers were only too glad to employ a mouser. Now puss wouldn't get as much as a paw inside most bakeries. Indeed, to quote a public relations executive from Rank Hovis McDougall Ltd: 'There is no way that any cats, mice, or other animals are going to get into our modern hygienic bakeries!' Poor Puss! However, rumour has it that a plump, contented puss named Tiger has managed to penetrate London's swanky Ritz hotel – on the pretext of course of keeping it mouse-free.

Still, the cat which, arguably, was the most 'famous' in recent years, was owned by a firm which certainly had milling interests, Spillers Ltd, whose white cat Arthur successfully promoted sales of their cat food until he died, just short of his seventeenth birthday, in March 1976. Arthur, the cat who scooped the Kattomeat product out of the tin with his/her paw, and started life as Samantha, led an exciting life culminating in a High Court action to determine his/her ownership. At one stage Arthur was even handed over for political asylum on the steps of the Russian Embassy. There was, too, the suggestion that his teeth had been taken out by Spillers, thus enabling him to eat so charmingly with his paw. This was nonsense, of course. Arthur had to have some teeth removed because of an ulcerated mouth. Between television and film engagements he lived a life of luxury in a first class cat hotel, and received fan mail from all over the world which was suitably answered by Spillers, signed with a facsimile of Arthur's own paw.

Another cat which commanded the respect and admiration of viewers was the Silver Persian, Lewishof, Michael of Jemari, the Kosset carpet promoter; and of course, there have been many other felines anonymous, fictional and otherwise, which have stolen scenes and hearts in full-length feature films, like Pywacket, the witch's cat in John van Druten's *Bell, Book and Candle*; the pathetic 'no-name' cat who shared Audrey Hepburn's flat in *Breakfast at Tiffany's*, and Tao, the Siamese in Walt Disney's *The Incredible Journey*, the story of a bull terrier, Labrador and Siamese cat who battle across Canada to rejoin their owners.

There is a Disney family fun film called *The Cat from Outer Space* about a mysterious cat who lands on earth in a spaceship which has developed engine trouble. The cat has strange powers and has all the staff at a US Air Force base doing just what it wishes, including repairing the spaceship.

And, of course, there is the Disney classic, *The Aristocats*. This is the tale of a cat family: Duchess, the mother, and her children, Marie, Toulouse and Berlioz, who are abandoned by the wicked butler, Edgar, whose plan it is to lose them when he hears his mistress making her will in favour of the cats; he is to inherit her fortune only when the cats are dead.

Thomas O'Malley, an alley cat, comes to their rescue, as does a little mouse called Roquefort and two farm dogs called Napoleon and Lafayette. It is an absolute must for cat lovers.

Practically every farmyard or riding stable has a 'mouser', to protect the feedstuffs from mice.

There is hardly a riding, or livery stable, which does not boast a stable cat, kept to protect the feedstuffs from mice, the cats usually forming a good relationship with the equines who remain undisturbed as the stable puss reclines blissfully on their straw. Like the farm cat, few of these moggies receive a retainer.

Another service, albeit unpaid, that numerous cats perform is that of companion to the artistic and famous. Former Prime Minister, Sir Harold Wilson, has a Siamese cat, and author, Beverley Nicholls, writes sympathetically of his, just as French novelist, Colette, did before him, about her precious La Chatte, and Samuel Johnson about Hodge, the cat with whom he shared his Fleet Street lodgings.

That distinguished actor, James Mason, who today, with his wife Clarissa is joint president of an educational trust called Animal Vigilantes, managed to repay in some measure the affection his beloved cats gave him when he was the leading film actor of the British screen; replying to his fans' requests for photos, he wrote that an autographed picture would be sent in return for a donation of 1s. in support of a cat charity, which benefited enormously.

There are cats who patrol back-stage and encourage performers at many of London's West End theatres. There is Ambrose at Drury Lane Theatre, Plug at the Adelphi and Bouncer at the Garrick. Perhaps, however, the most unusual and appealing story of a well-known moggy is that of Paddington Cat, or Tiddles, which was related for readers of the magazine, *Woman's Realm* recently, by journalist Sonia Roberts.

Tiddles was found, as a hungry stray kitten, on Paddington Station in the summer of 1970 by a Miss June Wilson who looks after the 'Ladies', and despite strenuous efforts to trace his owners they did not come forward. June and her colleagues adopted Tiddles and provided him with a basket and every comfort in the 'Ladies'. Tasty meals are prepared for him – in fact he now weighs 11.8 kg (26 lb) –

and every Christmas he receives his own presents and a tree. Through the years many admirers have written to Tiddles, care of Paddington Station, and his health is enquired after assiduously. Once it was suggested to June that station life was no life for a cat and Tiddles might prefer a real home. He didn't, and was soon back at Paddington Station sharing mousing duties with the cat in the Electrician's Department.

A bedraggled ship's cat, sharing the hardships of a cheerless fo'c'sle, and streaking ashore at foreign ports for a night on the local tiles, has always been an essential ingredient of any sea story. But alas, no more. Five years ago, the British Fleet were advised to land pets before sailing, following a tightening of protective measures against rabies.

What would happen to the luckless pets? Surely they would not be put down? A letter from Captain Tom Baird printed in *The Daily Telegraph* on 19 May 1975 put cat lover's minds at rest. He wrote:

'As the instigator of the instruction to the Fleet, as well as being a pet lover myself, and the owner of a black and white cat and a dog, not to mention a pony and a goat, I can assure other pet lovers that there is no intention of ships' pets being indiscriminately put to death, or turned loose to fend for themselves.'

'Sailors would not stand for that sort of thing anyway. The ship's cat in particular will continue to enjoy fair and sympathetic treatment (within the provisions of the new law) being traditionally recognized by 'Jack' as occupying the position at the end of the line for any blame handed down by higher authority.'

Seagoing cats were destined to become landlubbers, but it is pleasant to reminisce on their past glory.

Unique among ships' cats was Simon, a black and white tom, wounded on board the frigate *HMS Amethyst* when she was fired on in the Yangtse in April 1949. Despite injuries from shell blast – 'capable of making a hole over a foot in diameter in steel plates' – he helped to keep down the rats on board during the hundred days that the ship was detained in the river by the Chinese Communists.

In the badly damaged ship, Simon sailed down the Yangtse in the *Amethyst*, when she made her dramatic dash to freedom, and, on his return to Britain, was awarded the PDSA's Dickin Medal – regarded as the animals' Victoria Cross – 'for behaviour of the highest order throughout the action'.

A ship's cat which seemed to have the knack of getting his name in the papers was Fred Wunpound (Lucky Fred). Certainly he caused a stir when he filled in a census form.

He was described on the form as being born in England, of doubtful parentage, single and male. This didn't worry Fred. But it did puzzle Scotland's Registrar General, Mr Archibald Rennie, who was not to know that Fred was a cat and entitled to be included in the census because he was included on the ration strength of *HMS Hecate* based at Portsmouth, Hampshire.

His shipmates filled in the form for Fred . . . employed as the ship's 'mouser'. And to make it all legal, Fred signed the form with his paw.

Without Able Seacat Wunpound, mouser (second class), Scotland's population would have been 5,227,706.

Fred's release from sea-going duties was faithfully recorded in *Navy News* in July, 1975, with a quote from Vice-Admiral Tait that 'Wunpound, and his kind, will be sadly missed, not only by the ship's company of *HMS Hecate*, but the Fleet in general.' He linked the name of Wunpound with that of Hodge, Dr Johnson's cat, and thought that the redoubtable Doctor's words to Boswell could well have been attributed to Wunpound: 'Sir, he is a very fine cat, a very fine cat indeed.' And Wunpound, because of his excellent service at sea, was not recategorized as a 'shorecat'.

Even his death justified a generous mention in *The Daily Telegraph* in July 1976, when the following obituary appeared:
'The longest serving sailor aboard the Royal Navy survey ship *Hecate* has died at the age of ten. He was the ship's mousecatcher, Leading Seacat Wunpound.'

Pressed into service from the Plymouth RSPCA in 1966 for a bounty of £1, from which he took his name, Fred travelled over a quarter of a million miles (402,400 km) abroad until the new anti-rabies law made him 'swallow the anchor'.

Like every rating, he had a dossier of Official Service Documents. They show he gained promotion from Junior Hecat to Ordinary Hecat to Able Seacat, and qualified for a kit upkeep allowance.

At the time of his discharge he had two good conduct badges – and one disgraceful conduct badge, earned after an incident in the Brixham fishmarket!

Obviously he was a very fine cat, a very fine cat indeed!

Cat behaviour

Has it every occurred to you that the cat is the only domestic animal which, despite close association with man, has, through its intelligence, been able to ensure its own well-being and safety without falling victim to man's will? For three thousand years, the cat has patronized human households, used them, like a hotel, and today his existence is as detached and self-contained as it ever was. The cat lives its own life in the way that it chooses.

Maybe the reason why the cat is able to accept our hospitality and, unlike the dog, live its own life at the same time, is that its brain is similar to our own, except that it does not have the same facility for memory or speech and the brain of man has larger frontal lobes. The cat does, however, have eight senses: balance, direction, hearing, sight, smell, taste, time and touch; and it is possible that it experiences the same sensations as we do, since the cat's brain centre for feelings of anger, pleasure, sex and so on is almost identical to our own.

Physical characteristics

Cats have graceful and flexible bodies which make them very agile in their movements. The skeleton of the cat is made up of about 200 bones with more than 500 skeletal muscles.

As the shoulder joints are free a cat is able to turn its head easily and move its forelegs freely. The structure allows the back to be arched when the cat is frightened, and enables it to spring and jump without effort.

The skulls of all members of the feline family are much the same in shape, but vary tremendously in size. More than in humans, the teeth differ in different parts of the mouth. The most important are the fang-like canine teeth which enables a wild cat to seize and kill its prey and sometimes give a nasty bite when fighting.

The long tongue is covered with papillae. These are tiny little hooks which give the tongue a rasp-like feel and allow the cat to lick the meat off bones. The tongue is also used much like a face flannel for washing purposes. By first licking the paws the cat can clean itself all over. Of course, the tongue is also used for lapping up liquids.

The large beautiful eyes of most cats have pupils that expand or contract according to the amount of light, being mere slits in bright sunlight and wide open when there is scarcely any light.

Right: Whilst enjoying the warmth of the hearth, cats still manage to remain independent and slightly aloof.

26

This cat is having a good wash. By first licking her paws she can clean herself all over.

Cats have a third eyelid, known as the nictitating membrane – sometimes referred to as 'the haws'. This may be seen sometimes in the corners of the eyes when a cat is sickening for an illness or is run-down.

Some cats have large, pointed ears; others have small rounded ones. But all have acute hearing and many know when their owners are coming by recognizing their footsteps. Whistling attracts their attention though it is difficult to know whether they enjoy it or not.

The ears too, are a very good indication of a cat's moods. They are held high when the cat is pleased; but when flattened and close to the head, it usually means the cat is annoyed. A twitch of the ear may mean that a cat knows it has been called and prefers to take no notice. The head will be turned so that the ears face the direction of a sound which can thereby be heard better. Cats can hear very faint sounds, such as a mouse creeping through grass, or a mole digging underground.

The length of the nose is short in most cats and although the sense of smell is said to be less acute than that of dogs, it is still very good. A cat will normally refuse any food that has gone off. They usually prefer their food slightly warmed.

A cat's whiskers are much thicker and coarser than the hairs in the fur, and some cats have really magnificent specimens. They enable a cat to move around in the dark without bumping into things, and protect the eyes when hunting.

It has been said that the whiskers are used as a kind of measure, so that a cat knows whether or not it can squeeze through a small opening. This is doubtful, as most cats judge by sight.

Most cats have thick soft fur almost completely covering their bodies. The fur forms a protection against the weather by trapping a layer of air close to the skin. Some cats have two layers of fur; a soft undercoat and guard hairs. When a cat is frightened or angry it is the guard hairs that stand up, making the body look much bigger.

Cat usually lose their fur twice a year, in the spring and late autumn. This is a gradual process and is one of the reasons why grooming long-haired cats every day is so important. It helps to remove most of the loose hairs that may be licked down inside when the cat is washing. These may form a hair or furball and could cause trouble.

Tails vary in length and thickness; though the Manx cat does not have a tail. The long-hair cats have short, but very full tails; while those of the Siamese are long and thin, tapering to a point and covered with very short fur.

The tail, like the ears, is a good indication of a cat's moods. It can

Beware! Ears which are flattened and close to the head indicate that the cat is in a bad mood.

29

Left: Cats always manage to find the most comfortable place in which to sleep, but even when relaxing they remain alert to the slightest movement or sound.

be held high over the body when the cat is pleased; swished from side to side when it is cross, and twitched at the tip when very angry. (When a cat runs round and round chasing its own tail it is said to be a sign of a change in the weather.)

A cat can make a number of different sounds. The most curious is the purring when pleased. No-one is quite sure how this sound is made, but it is believed to happen when two vocal chords vibrate together. A mother cat will make a chirping, almost bird-like sound to her kittens, but will give a low growl to warn them if she thinks they are in danger. Cats can also swear, growl and spit when displeased or frightened.

Cats sleep a lot, but somehow rarely very deeply. They are always on the tiptoe of expectation and seem to know what is going on. They are intelligent and they are also independent.

Balance

The cat may not have the legendary nine lives as well as eight senses, but it does, on occasions, have miraculous escapes which can be accredited to its wonderful sense of balance. A human is likely to fall from a height as a dead weight; the cat, on the other hand, whether falling from just a little way or from a building, will twist its body so that it manages to land on four feet. It does, to quote, the noted veterinarian and animal behaviourist, Michael Fox, have a righting reflex, the extended legs being very resilient and acting as landing pads to reduce the chances of the cat sustaining a severe back or internal injury. Let your cat fall from your arms and you will see how it twists its body and lands firm.

Cats have a good sense of balance and do generally land on their feet. In spite of this, many are sometimes badly injured falling from roofs and windows, so if you live in a flat, it is a good idea to wire-in balconies if they are very high up and the cat is in the habit of lying outside. It's better to be safe than to be sorry!

Direction

My husband likes to tell the tale of a family pet cat who, given a new home by neighbours when his parents moved from London to Brighton, turned up three weeks later at the door of their new Brighton home. On a humbler level I was amazed, and delighted, when our lilac-point Siamese asked to be let out within an hour of arrival at our new home, wandered cautiously round the precincts, then presented himself at the window for re-admittance, a procedure he followed for the next few days, staying out for longer periods on each occasion until he obviously felt secure as to his whereabouts.

The cat has, like the carrier pigeon, an uncanny homing device. Some say this is because of its exquisite sense of timing and that it can find its way according to the position of the sun; others attribute this facility to clairvoyance, the supernatural power from which cats can never really be disassociated.

Hearing

The sensitivity of dogs and cats to sound does not differ greatly from that of man. However, at frequencies over 500 Hz their ability is superior to our own.

Michael Fox, in his book *Understanding your Cat*, says that cats can discriminate with 75 per cent accuracy between two sound sources separated by an angle of 5 degrees, a performance on the same order as man's. But the cat has the advantage of having a mobile

Although cats have a good sense of balance, it is a good idea to keep an eye on very young kittens to make sure they don't get into too much trouble.

32

external ear, or pinna, which it can use to collect sound waves and also scan the environment or direct it attention to a particular source of sound.

Do cats communicate vocally with individuals and with each other? Normally vocal communication is limited to the purr of contentment, yowl of pain or anger and the domestic meow for attention: 'Let me in, please!'; but as cats tend to be solitary animals there seems little vocal play between them except for the caterwauling during courtship, the call to battle between toms and the mating cry of the queen.

The Siamese, of course, is renowned for its 'call' which delights the breed devotee, but can put off the peace-loving. My Siamese will growl if the dogs approach his food bowl; also with pleasure if a tasty piece of fish has been presented. He will answer when called, carry on a conversation, calling on cue, and when reprimanded, always insists that he has the last word.

The Siamese owner will confirm that their cat has a call to specially express the whole gamut of emotions: pleasure, anger, hunger, and simply when it just wants attention. It is a talkative animal which likes the sound of its own voice. The Siamese cat owner never feels alone!

Sight

Earlier I mentioned how the Egyptians noticed that the pupils of a cat's eyes altered according to the changing light and thought this to be magic. It was their belief that, during the hours of darkness, the

The pupils of a cat's eyes contract and expand according to the strength of the light, but they cannot see in the dark.

cat's eyes still reflected the sun, their sun god, 'Ra', in the form of a cat, working against the evil powers of darkness.

The cat is unable to see in the dark, but the pupils of its eyes contract or expand according to the strength of light and they are responsive to the merest chink of brightness. At night the pupils dilate, in daylight they diminish to the narrowest slit. If you look at a cat you will see that its eyes are centrally positioned on the head, unlike those of, for instance, the horse, which are on the side. This facility enables the cat to measure distance more accurately.

It is fascinating to watch a cat in concentration, for the pupils change shape as the cat measures the distance to its prey. Incidentally, it was believed until fairly recent times that the cat, like the dog, could see only in shades of black, white and grey. Now we understand that, if not in glorious technicolor, the cat can see certainly in diffused shades of red, green and blue.

Smell

The cat, like the dog, has a scenting facility superior to man. Both animals have what is known as a vomeronasal organ enabling it, via two ducts situated in the palate behind the upper incisor teeth, to draw odours from certain substances via the mouth to the olfactory organ. The territory marking of a cat, the scent of another cat; such odours undetected by humans can be drawn by the cat and dog into the organ and influence their behaviour.

Sound and scent are associated with the pleasure of taste and food; nothing, in fact, brings a cat running faster than the smell of kippers in the fry-pan coupled with the banging of a spoon against a saucer at the door. Familiar sounds and smells are linked with a sequence of events.

Time

The cat is able to navigate, using the sun as a compass, and its timing is usually dead accurate. The cat accustomed to its owner arriving home from the office at 5.30 pm will habitually be waiting at the door, or rushing down the path to meet him. It is aware of its master's time of rising, retiring and mealtimes. The only occasion when inaccuracies occur is when the hour goes back or forward which, in fairness, also bemuses horses and other livestock who wait at what is, after all, their customary hour, to be fed or led back to their stabling.

Touch

The strongest instinct, albeit closely followed by the need for food, is affection: the touch and comfort of the mother, the continuance and reassurance of touch. The cat is particularly sensual and adores being petted – my own cat purrs, in anticipation of a caress, as soon as an approach is made in his direction.

Right: Cats often anticipate their owner's arrival home from work at the customary time.

Opposite page: Cats love to be stroked and petted. This adoring owner lavishes her love on her new kitten.

The mother (or queen) will clean the kitten, an action which is almost a caress, and later, the cat will solicit this touch, or stroke, from its owner; will rub its head, or tail against them as an act of friendship, and maybe to mark his territorial right with an undetected scent from the temporal gland. Experiments among cats, dogs, and humans too, have proved the importance of the old-fashioned, age-old emotion *love*. You can feed and care for the young pet or human with the utmost diligence, but deprived of love, and the comfort of touch, they may survive but will certainly never attain their true potential.

Relationships

Unlike the dog, which through process of domestication has lost the power to fend for itself, the cat, even the pedigree, cut off from home comforts, will revert to the wild and become what is known as a feral cat (a domestic cat that has gone wild), hunting for food and rearing its young in the great outdoors.

Redevelopment areas often produce such unhappy feral families; their human owners having been rehoused in flats where they are

Left: Many cats are discarded by their owners, who had not considered that the sweet kitten would one day become a fully-grown cat. These cats, left to fend for themselves, will revert to their wild state.

Below: Kittens love to play together.

precluded from pet-keeping. Rather than seek the help of the Cats' Protection League or asking a vet to put their pet painlessly to sleep, they abandon it to take its chance with others. How often have you seen an old lady with a string bag of goodies feeding feral cats in the grounds of some old churchyard or derelict railway siding, the pretty kittens, which one longs to stroke, as fierce as tigers in miniature?

The dog, in its wild state, is a pack animal and retains this instinct to the extent that, where a number of males are kept, one dog will emerge as the leader, with a second in order of precedence; similarly a stallion will lead and protect its equine herd. The cat, on the other hand, is a solitary animal which will avoid other cats if it can and, when faced with an unavoidable encounter, will step aside to let a younger, and stronger cat, pass. This way he may avoid the fight a head-on meeting could entail.

Cats living in the same household will generally develop a relationship, the kittens playing tirelessly together and grooming each other assiduously in later years.

Intrusion by a new cat into a household is resented, but there are exceptions. Some years ago, we inherited, when we bought a country house, an honest-to-goodness tabby cat called Vicky, born at a nearby farm. We had her spayed, welcomed her to the fireside, and expected her to be a long-term companion. At that time we had a Chihuahua pup, with whom she showed much tolerance, and we certainly had no intention of buying another cat until we found ourselves visiting kennels on business; the proprietors bred Siamese, and my husband, a lifelong devotee, was entranced. We came home with Samson, our lilac-point. Vicky growled at first, then decided to tolerate the young newcomer . . . as long as he kept a respectful distance.

Slowly the situation improved until, to my surprise, I noticed that Vicky was schooling our kitten in the manner of a queen with her family; teaching Samson, among other things, the trick of skilfully walking backwards along the window sill to find the open pane.

One day, on going upstairs to our bedroom, I found Vicky sitting serenely on the bed, Samson beside her. They both looked so content I could not disturb them. Next morning, Vicky, the cat we had not sought, but thought would be with us for years, was run over. I have wondered often if Vicky had some uncanny forewarning that she would be leaving us, and groomed Samson, in advance, to take her place.

Territorial rights

The young tom cat whose owners move to a new neighbourhood faces problems akin to a new boy at school. He has to fight to prove himself, an exercise which can result in severe injuries if there happens to be a bigger, stronger tom next door who may well challenge him.

The tom, especially if unneutered, sprays urine, thereby leaving a scent on trees, shrubs, even furniture to mark out his territory. Territorial marking is, however, not confined to toms; nor is the scent always so strong. Indeed, the friendly 'marking' made by a cat when it rubs its head against our leg is just his, or her, harmless way of saying that we are 'their' home territory, but it is nonetheless a scent mark made with the scent glands of the tail, head and lips.

Cats will stop and sniff the marking of other cats, and maybe make their mark in return, rather like the presentation of a visiting card. Scientists may yet be able to prove that, from the mark or scent, cats can determine the age, sex and other information about the visitor, but that is as yet in the future.

Cat-and-mouse behaviour

Kittens enjoy nothing better than playing with a piece of paper tied on a string, but have you ever stopped to think that you are teaching it how to hunt, stalk and pounce on its prey? You are, but do not stop, because play is an essential for kittens. The young animal, or child, who is forbidden play and exertion may grow up with severe inhibitions.

The queen, in the wild, will present her kittens with a dead mouse for dinner; later this will be replaced with a live offering which they will be invited to stalk and kill, the final *'coup de grâce'* being a neck bite which severs the victim's spinal cord. The accomplished terrier kills similarly but with a characteristic shake of the head.

Some folk are put off keeping a cat because of its alleged cruelty, the slow 'cat-and-mouse' torture play prior to kill. The cat is, however, following its normal instinct for survival, an instinct which, in the cat, has not been extinguished by domesticity.

An interesting point is, that in experiments where kittens have been raised with mice, few took to killing them in later life. And, despite oft-told tales about the 'cat and the canary', a housecat often will live in harmony with a natural enemy.

I have sometimes come home to find a dead, half-devoured wild rabbit in a corner. Conversely my Siamese will treat as a friend, and share a run and a game with a pet doe rabbit, confirming the belief of myself, and many others, that all creatures, regardless of species, will get on with each other, if introduced from a sufficiently early age.

A cat's life

Cat behaviour becomes interrelated with human behaviour when one asks: 'Why do you own, or want to own a cat?' Very often, apart from wanting to love and own a thing of beauty, it is to fulfil some need in ourselves; the cat is required to be, as so often is the case with a pet dog, a love object to take the place of the missing husband, wife, or mother; someone to come home to at the end of a working day; a living companion for the lonely. If this is true, there is no harm in it. Doubtless you and the cat will thrive in each other's company. The cat may also perform a valuable function for the

Above: By catching birds and mice, cats are following their natural instincts for survival.

Right: A cat-flap will stop your cat from being a prisoner in the home while you are at work all day.

lonely, providing the incentive for that person to buy food and provide warmth of which they might deprive themselves if fending only for their own needs.

But the cat must not be regarded as a human zombie. It must be allowed freedom and an independent existence. In my early twenties I shared a bedsitter with a ginger cat who, for months, I was reluctant to let out the window. Eventually, friends said rightly: 'Don't keep him prisoner.' That is what the cat had become because of my over-protectiveness.

The unspayed queen, or undoctored tom, that is forcibly

restrained from hunting, or seeking a mate, may become aggressive, resentful and even destructive. Neutering and spaying will cut short the cat's instinct for sexual activity thereby making it contented and homeloving, a more satisfied and satisfying domestic pet. Don't nurture the view that, by keeping a pet tom entire or female unspayed you are allowing it to lead a normal life; not if you want it to be a full-time fireside companion. You can't have it both ways!

It is also important to choose a cat whose personality and characteristics suit your own. The Devon Rex is playful and mischievous, the Siamese trainable and dog-like. You can even teach it to walk beside you on a lead!

Breeds of cats

Nothing is more praiseworthy than to give a home to a pet cat especially if it otherwise faces destruction. Many pet lovers do, however, experience disappointment, when having rushed out and bought the first cat, dog, or even pet rabbit or guinea pig they see advertised, they discover too late the wide choice of types they might have chosen from had they gone into their purchase more carefully.

The best way to choose a pet is to look though a book like this, which has lots of illustrations, decide the breeds which take your fancy – for instance most people have a preference for either long-coated or short-coated varieties, and then visit a cat show in your area where you will have a chance to talk to cat breeders and find out if, and when, kittens of the type you most like are available. Cat breeders are not unscrupulous people out to take your money. Most likely they began by excitedly purchasing their first pedigree kitten just as you are doing, became interested in the breed, and gradually discovered the pleasure of breeding and showing.

In Britain, you will be able to find out when cat shows are being held in your area by ordering the newspaper, *Fur and Feather* from your newsagent, or by writing (enclosing a stamped addressed envelope), to The Secretary, Governing Council of the Cat Fancy, Dovefields, Petworth Road, Witley, Surrey. The Council can also advise on specialist cat clubs and societies; these are, for instance, clubs catering for the needs of almost every pedigree variety, as well as general regional cat clubs. Best known venue of the Cat Fancy is of course the National Cat Club Show, which is held at Olympia, west London, in December.

Listed is a schedule of the pedigree cat varieties with their breed numbers allocated by the Governing Council of The Cat Fancy. Basically, breeders found that by mating different cats together new kinds could be made. Today these are divided into two main sections; cats with long fur, whose ancestors came from Ankara (then Angora) in Turkey and Iran (then Persia); and those with short fur.

Cats with short coats are again divided:

1 Those with short fur, round heads, big rounded eyes and shortish thick tails, known as British cats (said to be descended from the cats that came with the Romans).

2 Foreign short-hairs, with longish heads, almond-shaped eyes, and long thin tails, which came in the first place from cats brought from the Far East.
3 Siamese, of similar shape, but having pale fur on the bodies and dark faces, ears, legs and tails.
4 The Rex, slim cats, but unusual in that the fur is very short and curly.

Pedigree cats

Long-haired cats

Breed number	Official breed name
1	Black
2	Blue-eyed White
2 a	Orange-eyed White
2 b	Odd-eyed White
3	Blue
4	Red Self
5	Cream
6	Smoke
6 a	Blue Smoke
7	Silver Tabby
8	Brown Tabby
9	Red Tabby
10	Chinchilla
11	Tortoiseshell
12	Tortoiseshell-and-white
12 a	Bi-colour
13	Blue-cream
13 b	Colourpoint
13 c	Birman
13 d	Turkish

Siamese

Breed number	Official breed name
24	Seal-point Siamese
24 a	Blue-point Siamese
24 b	Chocolate-point Siamese
24 c	Lilac-point Siamese
32	Tabby-point Siamese
32 a	Red-point Siamese
32 b	Tortoiseshell-point Siamese
32 c	Cream-point Siamese

Short-haired cats

Breed number	Official breed name
14	Blue-eyed White
14 a	Orange-eyed White
14 b	Odd-eyed White
15	Black

Short-haired cats *continued*

Breed number	Official breed name
16	British Blue
16 a	Russian Blue
17	Cream
18	Silver Tabby
19	Red Tabby
20	Brown Tabby
21	Tortoiseshell
22	Tortoiseshell-and-white
23	Abyssinian
23 a	Red Abyssinian
23 x	Blue Abyssinian
25	Manx
25 a	Stumpie Manx
25 b	Tailed Manx
27	Brown Burmese
27 a	Blue Burmese
27 b	Chocolate Burmese
27 c	Lilac Burmese
27 d	Red Burmese
27 e	Tortoiseshell Burmese
27 f	Cream Burmese
27 g	Blue-cream Burmese
27 h	Chocolate Tortoiseshell Burmese
27 j	Lilac Tortoiseshell Burmese
28	Blue-cream
29	Havana
29 c	Foreign Lilac
30	Spotted
31	Bi-colour
33	Cornish Rex
33 a	Devon Rex
34	Korat
35	Foreign White
36	Smoke
37	Foreign Black
38	Oriental Spotted Tabby
39	British Tipped

NB For explanation of breed numbers, *see* Chapter 6.

Over eighty breeds of cats, including colour varieties, are recognized today, most of which have developed in the last thirty years. Only a handful are of ancient origin: the best known is the original seal-point Siamese, from which several other colour-points have been produced by selective breeding. Even now, however, only about 5 per cent of British cats can boast a pedigree and most of these are Siamese, Burmese (developed in the 1930s in the USA!) or Abyssinian (developed in Britain, possibly from a cat brought back from Abyssinia in 1868).

Crossbred 'moggy' cats come in a wide variety of colours, with virtually all tortoiseshell cats female, but not all ginger cats male. Genetically, short-coats are dominant to long-coats, so most moggies are short-coated.

Siamese cats

The Siamese is the most popular of the pedigree cats, with body fur of pale cream and darker coloured face, ears, paws and tail. The head is wedge-shaped with a long nose, big ears and bright blue almond-shaped eyes. The kittens are nearly white when first born, with the darker colouring (known as the points) only showing after a few weeks.

The points colourings range from seal brown to cream. The Siamese was said to have come from the Royal Palace in Bangkok, Thailand, nearly a hundred years, ago. However, Siamese expert, May Dunnill, in her *Siamese Cat Owners' Encyclopedia*, states that they may have descended from a cat seen in the 1700s by Peter Simon Pallas, a German explorer and naturalist, in the area of the Caspian Sea. This cat was said to be the progeny of a black cat and had a light chestnut-brown body colour, black at the back and paler along the sides and belly, with a black streak running along and surrounding the eyes, ending at the front of the forehead. The ears, paws and tail were black and 'the head longer towards the nose' than that of the common cat. Mrs Dunnill adds that a picture in Pallas' book shows a cat with the Siamese coat pattern.

The Siamese is the most dog-like of the cats and arguably the most dependable. He loves his owners, gets on well with other pets, and is miserable if left alone. He comes when called, can be trained to walk on a lead and is keenly intelligent. He is also adept and persistent at obtaining his own way, 'calling' in his distinctive voice until he gets it.

Siamese have a reputation, undeserved, for destructiveness – a gentle tap on the paws of an offending kitten and the provision of a scratching post will prevent this. They are gentle with children and adore being groomed. Just watch that tail bush out with pleasure! Kittens can be a little timid until you have won their love and confidence. You could even find one hiding in the chimney!

Red-point Siamese

These cats have been bred for at least fifteen years and received official recognition by the Governing Council of the Cat Fancy in 1966. A first step in their production was a cross between the

seal-point Siamese and the Red Tabby Short-hair. The points colour is red-golden, to my eye a glorious marmalade.

Tortoiseshell-point Siamese

This variety was officially recognized in 1966 but has been in existence for at least fifteen years. The tortie points were originally produced by a cross between seal-point Siamese and Red Tabby Short-hair. Tortie points when suitably mated can produce any colour Siamese.

Seal-point Siamese

The seal-point was first introduced in Britain in 1884 and is now the most popular of all pedigree varieties. The kittens are born white, or cream coloured, with the points appearing in a few days. Body colour is cream, with dark seal-brown points. The Siamese has typical foreign characteristics, a long *svelte* body on slim legs, small oval feet, wedge-shaped head with straight nose, large pricked ears, deep blue eyes and long tapering tail. Squints and badly kinked tails are not allowed.

Blue-point Siamese

Cat requirements are as for other Siamese. The body colour should be glacier white and the points blue. Many cats of this variety show a suffusion of fawn on the body colour and this is considered to be a bad fault.

Chocolate-point Siamese

Typical Siamese characteristics are required as for other coloured varieties of Siamese, i.e. long lithe bodies, wedge-shaped heads with fine muzzles, large pointed ears, dainty small feet and oriental-shaped eyes of vivid blue. The body colour should be ivory with points of milk chocolate.

Opposite page: Each Siamese variety is distinguished by the colour of the points. Siamese kittens are born white, the points developing as they grow older. This is a tabby-point Siamese.

Left: Pictured here are two well-known varieties of Siamese: on the left, the lilac-point and on the right, the chocolate-point.

Lilac-point Siamese

This variety is increasing considerably in numbers and proving to be very popular. The type is as for other Siamese with body colouring of frosty white and points of delicate lilac grey. The pads are pink and the nose a faded rose, with eyes of vivid blue. The coloration is due to the presence of the genes giving chocolate and blue, and in some lights the points appear to be pink.

There is also a cream-point Siamese which is relatively new on the scene.

The Balinese Cat

The question most often asked at shows and among cat fanciers is 'what is the difference between the Balinese and the Colourpoint, or as it is called in the USA, Himalayan?' The Himalayan, well known across the country as the Colourpoint, is a Persian type cat with Siamese colouring. As such, it is judged by the Persian standard (short cobby body, wide head, short nose, short tail, round eyes with a sweet expression). It was developed by Mrs Marguerita Goforth of La Mesa, California, USA, who crossed Persians with Siamese and worked for many years to perfect this beautiful cat with its rich Persian coat.

The Balinese, on the other hand, is a pure Siamese cat. No other breed has been crossed with it to achieve the long coat. Consequently it is judged by the Siamese standard (body long and lithe, long legs and tail, almond-shaped eyes, wedge-shaped head), the only difference is that the Balinese has long, very soft, silky hair. This long hair has come from mutations, that is to say, long-haired kittens have turned up spontaneously among pure-bred, pedigree Siamese litters. These unusual kittens have been treasured by a few breeders and by carefully breeding long-haired Siamese to long-haired Siamese they proved that the cats will breed true, all long-haired. The Balinese make the most perfect pets one could wish for.

The coats of this breed, or so the Balinese Society tell us, are much easier to keep in order than most long-hairs as they are more flowing, not so dense and do not mat. Also they do not shed, even as much as short-hairs. Depending on the climate in your area, they may shed briefly, once a year; but most of the time you can wear black or navy blue with impunity even if your home boasts several Balinese.

They are very intelligent and lively cats and, like their Siamese forebears, enjoy taking part in their owner's activities. They tend to be quieter than the average Siamese. Not to say they aren't chatty when spoken to. You will always get a response from these long-haired Siamese; but you will get fewer demands. They are wonderfully gentle and affectionate. It is said that you never get a mean one.

The Balinese Society was formed in Britain in August 1978 with the purpose of safeguarding and promoting the pure-breeding of Balinese cats. The Balinese is by definition a long-haired Siamese. No other breed must be introduced. The Balinese coat, which is long, fine and silky, lying flat and flowing towards the rear, comes from natural mutations.

The temperament should be typically happy, lively and affectionate, not restless or always meowing, and the ideal Balinese should make an excellent, practical, healthy pet, easy to handle, easy to care for and, easy to love.

Long-haired Cats

The Turkish Cat
These attractive cats differ from other long-hairs in that their heads are longer, the ears bigger and the fur not so long. Their fur is pure white with auburn, that is reddish, markings, on the heads and tails. Their eyes are amber in colour.

They are said to be very like the first long-hairs that came to Britain from Turkey a long time ago, where they enjoyed swimming in warm pools and streams. They were once called Angoras and are still known in Turkey today. In fact, they are being bred in a zoo in Ankara – the modern name of Angora.

The White Long-hair
A really lovely white with a beautiful long pure white coat and good tail. The head is broad and round, the ears small, and big eyes a deep orange colour. Sometimes Whites have blue eyes, or even one eye orange and one eye blue. The variety has been known as the blue-eyed white, the orange-eyed white and the odd-eyed white.

These cats too originated in Turkey and were known as Angora after the city (now Ankara) but as they came to Britain from France

Above: The White Long-Hair (Persian) has big eyes a deep orange-colour.

Left: The Odd-eyed White Long-hair. One eye is blue, the other orange or copper. There is also an Odd-eyed Short-hair variety. Take care that the cat you choose is not deaf on the blue-eyed side.

51

they were also known as French cats. In the early days the cats were thought to have an unresponsive temperament until it was discovered that they were deaf. Fortunately, crossbreeding has almost eliminated this disability but deafness does still occur particularly among the blue-eyed specimens, and where deafness manifests itself in the odd-eyed variety it is generally the blue-eyed side that is affected.

The Odd-eyed White may not represent everyone's idea of beauty but the sight of a glorious long-coated white cat, with one magnificent blue eye, the other a perfect orange, is a fascinating sight to behold, worthy of at least a second glance.

The Blue Long-hair

The Blue is often known as the Blue Persian (it was said that they first came from Persia long ago). They are the most popular of the cats with long coats. Their fur is a bluish-grey in colour, and may be a light or dark shade; but it must always be the same colour down to the roots. There must be no white hairs in the fur.

The heads are round, noses are broad and short, the ears small, eyes are a deep copper or orange colour. The tails are short but profuse. The kittens may be born with tabby markings which vanish as the fur grows. They make delightful pets.

The Tortoiseshell Long-hair

The Long-haired Tortoiseshell has a beautiful coat of red, cream and black and appears to be an entirely female variety which, according to international cat judge, Mrs Grace Pond, appears to have little proven history, produced, as it were, by luck more than anything else. It should have a coat of bright red and cream patches, interspersed with black. The colours should be in separate patches spread all over the body, including the face, ears, legs, paws, tail

The Blue Long-hair, often known as the Blue Persian.

and under the stomach. The patching must not be too large and should be of clear colours without white hairs or brindling. A cream or red mark, known as a blaze, running down from the forehead to the nose, is liked and does add character to the face. Large, wide open, copper or deep orange eyes set well apart are much sought after.

The Tortoiseshell-and-white Long-hair
This is a very attractive cat with a coat of red, black and cream patches, with some white. The head is broad, with big round eyes. Tortie-and-whites are always female and may have many different coloured kittens.

Long-haired Tabbies

The Brown Tabby Long-hair
This is one of the oldest varieties known, although there are now very few. Their coats are brown with black tabby markings which should form a certain pattern. On the head these look like a large 'M' with pencil markings around the eyes and on the cheeks. Looking down on the back the markings may make the shape of a large butterfly. There are also Silver Tabbies and Red Tabbies, the name, incidentally, being taken from Attabiya in Baghdad in Iraq. This was the district where many centuries ago, a silk, known in Britain as Tabbisilk, was produced, and because these cats bore a similar pattern they were known henceforth as tabby cats.

The Colourpoint Long-hair
The Colourpoint is a supremely magnificent cat, intelligent, affectionate and with a dog-like devotion to its human owner. Colourpoints are very individual in temperament, each differing from another. They are more enterprising in adult life than the average self-coloured Persian and, according to the Colourpoint Society of Great Britain, far less domineering and boisterous than the Siamese. Colourpoints make the most perfect pets and are to be had in several attractive point colours, such as seal, blue, chocolate, lilac, tortie, red and cream.

Colourpoints were first recognized in this country as a true breeding variety of cat in 1955. Some eight years of intensive breeding in Britain was expended on their production before that date, largely by the late Mr B. A. Stirling-Webb. Colourpoints have turned up by chance matings among domesticated cats in different parts of the world, but the fine specimens seen on show benches today have not originated in that manner. At earlier dates during this century attempts had been made to create long-haired, or Persian cats, with the colouring of Siamese, but no stable lineages were produced. The object of Colourpoint breeding is to produce a Persian cat with as fine a type as exists in the best self-coloured varieties, but with a colour pattern and blue eyes of the Siamese.

Similar cats, called Himalayans, were being produced in California, USA, at the same time as Colourpoints were being developed in Britain, the breeders then being unknown to each

Right: A Red Tabby Persian. His coat is a much truer red than that of the ginger tom housepet. But don't believe it when folk say that all red-coated cats are toms. It isn't so!

Opposite page: An unusual variety, the Persian cameo tabby.

other and hence the difference in the names of the cats. In the USA recognition of their Himalayans came in 1957. Colourpoints are not produced by a simple cross between a Persian and a Siamese. Such a mating results in self or even coloured short-haired cats, which, however, carry invisibly the heritable factors for long-hair and for the Siamese colour pattern. When two such carriers are mated together and many litters produced, one kitten in thirty-two, on the average, will show the Siamese pattern, blue eyes and long hair. This primitive Colourpoint breeds true, but it has much too long a nose and tall upright ears to pass for a good Persian cat.

Above: The Blue-point Colourpoint.

Right: The Red-point Colourpoint, one of the most beautiful of the long-hair varieties. It is dog-like as is the Siamese, but has a quiet, less demanding nature.

A Colourpoint is not at all a long-haired Siamese. Much time, work and money has been expended upon eliminating the unwanted Siamese features introduced into the primitive Colourpoint from its Siamese forebears, so producing the fine Persian type seen in our best specimens today.

The accepted standard for the Colourpoint Long-hair cat requires good Persian type with well-defined colour to the points, i.e. the mask, paws, and tail, and pale body colour. The head should be round and wide with a short, well-demarcated nose, broad cheeks, small, outwardly directed ears with good width between them. The body should be short and wide with short legs, wide paws and short full tail. In winter a fine frill should frame the face and the coat should be long and silky. The eyes are round and the bluer the better. Any resemblance in type to the Siamese is considered to be a fault.

Good type in Colourpoints has been achieved by mating Colourpoint to Colourpoint and selecting at each generation the best offspring for future breeding. But good type has been produced more speedily, although in fewer numbers, by outcrossing Colourpoints to the finest self-coloured Persians. The resulting self-coloured carriers may be as fine as the Persian parent and when mated back to Colourpoints produce some much finer Colourpoints and more carriers. Both methods of breeding are in use.

Colourpoints are hardy when adult, but must be kept warm as kittens. They thrive best on plenty of liberty, but if at all possible must be kept away from roads with their ceaseless toll in feline lives. Each one selects his own particular occupations and they need plenty of company and affection from their owners. Kittens particularly need human companionship. Whether your Colourpoint loves you or not depends upon you, but he is prepared to do so, in full measure. But if you reap the extreme pleasure of such an animal's devotion remember that it cannot easily be broken and should be taken on for the life of your pet.

The Birman Cat

To appreciate the legend which is about to be told, one must visualize the beautiful temples in the ancient land of Burma. The magnitude of the Buddha idols helps to impress upon us the deep religious faith the people have. Their belief in the reincarnation of souls and their deep respect and love for their priests provide the setting for this legend. Their watchful and loving care of the hundred white cats (Temple Cats) is due to their belief that the priests are returned to the temple in the form of the sacred cats of Burma known as Birman Cats. The origin of the whitegloved feet and the colouring goes back to before the birth of Christ.

Centuries ago the Khmer people of Asia built beautiful temples of worship to pay homage to their gods. The temple of Lao-Tsun housed a beautiful golden goddess with sapphire blue eyes, who watched over the transmutation of souls. Mun-Ha, one of the most beloved of the priests, whose beard had been braided with gold by the great god Son-Hio, often knelt in meditation before the golden goddess Tsun-Kyan-Kse. Sinh, a beautiful and faithful white temple cat, was always at his side, and shared his meditations. As the holy priest prayed, the sacred cat would gaze at the brilliant goddess. One night as the moon rose and Mun-Ha was kneeling before the sacred goddess, raiders attacked the temple and Mun-Ha was killed. At the moment of Mun-Ha's death, Sinh placed his feet upon his fallen master and faced the golden goddess. Immediately the hairs of his white body were as golden as the light radiating from the beautiful golden goddess, her beautiful blue eyes became his very own, and his four white legs shaded downwards to a velvety brown; but where his feet rested gently on his dead master, the whiteness remained white, thus denoting their purity.

The next morning the temple radiated with the transformation of the hundred white cats, which, like Sinh, reflected the golden hue of sunset. Sinh, the golden cat of Burma, never left the throne after his master's death. Then seven days later he too died, carrying with him into paradise the soul of Mun-Ha his beloved master.

Since that time, the followers of Buddhism guard very carefully and gently the sacred ones within whose bodies live their beloved priests. Only a few (and they must be worthy in deed and manner)

The Birman cat is instantly recognized by its white paws. The origin of this temple cat goes back to a time before the birth of Christ.

are permitted to possess one of these beautiful creatures. The people lived peacefully till the advent of Brahminism. The Brahmins felt that the Kittahs (priests) were practising a false religion, so they raided the temples and killed many venerable priests.

At this time two men, August Pavie and Major Gordon-Russell, two Englishmen who were residing in France at the time, journeyed from France to Burma. They were able to penetrate and bring protection to the lost Kittahs against the aggressive Brahmins. They were then able to see the hundred sacred cats and learn their legend.

Many of the Kittahs escaped and crossed the mountains of Burma into Tibet, taking with them their sacred cats. They then formed a new subterranean temple of Lao-Tsun, the dwelling place of their gods. This temple is a marvel of marvels in Indo-China. Not far from a lake, it is hidden in a mass of immense peaks.

The two men returned to France, and because of the great love the Burmese people had for August Pavie and Major Gordon-Russell, who had protected them against their enemy, a pair of the sacred cats was sent from the beautiful temple of Lao-Tsun to France, as a gesture of gratitude, in 1919. The ocean trip proved tragic however, for the male died. But it was found that the female was pregnant and thus the breed survived and became recognized in France in 1925.

The French breeders also had troubles of their own as, at the end of the Second World War only one pair of these sacred cats of Burma was left. The name Birman is derived from the French. (Burmese cats are totally unrelated).

These cats have a wonderful temperament. They are sweet, gentle and very loving with a small voice. And they are very beautiful. They walk with a tiger-like gait. They should have deep blue eyes, long-haired coats and points like the Siamese; but with four white feet, on the back legs ending in a gauntlet-like spur, reaching to the first joint.

There are now blue Birmans as well as seal Birmans.

In the seal-point, the body fur is a clear pale beige, slightly golden, with dark brown points, and in the blue-point Birman the body fur is bluish-white, rather cold in tone with blue-grey points. Chocolate-brown and lilac-point Birmans are also now appearing. The Birman has a longer body than most long-haired cats and its head is not so broad.

The Chinchilla Cat

The Chinchilla is one of the prettiest of cats with long coats and is often spoken of as the glamour girl of the cat world, the pure white fur being tipped with black giving almost a fairy-like look. The head is broad, with small ears, and the eyes a beautiful sea-green colour.

The kittens are dark when first born and it is hard to believe that they will soon grow into such beauties. They make delightful pets but it should be remembered that their long coats need some grooming every day.

The Red Self Long-hair

The Red Self Long-hair is a beautiful cat with a broad round head, small ears, short nose and big, round, deep copper coloured eyes, a problem with this variety being that there are usually tabby markings somewhere on the body which, for show purposes, are considered a fault. At one time the colour of these long-hairs was referred to as orange, and references to this colour appeared in show reports.

It is believed, however, that these early cats did not boast the beautiful red self-colour of today's long-hairs. There are also cream, smoke and blue smoke long-haired varieties; the Smoke looks almost black and it is only when the cat moves that the white undercoat is detected. The blue smoke also has a white undercoat, the blue colour taking the place of the black, while the cream is pure self-coloured.

The Blue-Cream Long-hair

The Blue-Cream has been evolved through the mating of Blue and Cream Long-hairs, sometimes the mating of a Tortoiseshell with a Blue or Black Long-hair. Breeders in Britain have gone to immense trouble to obtain the coat of soft and good texture of blue and cream intermingled. This is the required standard in Britain and in Europe but the coat patched, as in the tortoiseshell, is liked in the USA.

The required colours should be pale pastel shades without any trace of red, and, as with so many other breeds, patching is considered a fault. This is a cobby cat with a broad round head and tiny ears, and what looks like a gentleman's beautiful side whiskers. Again most Blue-Creams are feminine so crossbreeding is necessary to ensure continuity, usually by mating a cream female to a blue male.

The Bi-Colour Long-hair

At the turn of the century short-haired bi-coloured cats were being shown, and a list of acceptable colours that could combine with white were set down by Mr Harrison Weir, but the long-haired bi-colours had to be shown in any other colour classes, being black and white, blue and white, orange and white, and tabby and white. Bi-coloured cats have been seen in Britain for many years and generally acquired as pets. It was not until 1966, following the discovery that by selective breeding they might assist in the breeding of Tortoiseshell-and-whites, that a standard was granted by the Governing Council of the Cat Fancy based on Dutch rabbit marking. It will have been noticed that the cat and rabbit varieties have many similar names and groupings. Indeed the newspaper *Fur and Feather* caters for fanciers of both animals.

The Black Cat

The Black Cat was, in the Middle Ages, thought to be a creature of evil, the instrument of Satan. Nowadays, it is an omen of good luck and we believe that good fortune will befall us if a self-coloured black cat should happen to cross our path. Short-haired Black cats are, however, more frequently seen than the long-haired variety. The broad-headed Long-haired Black with its blazing orange eyes and, questionably, sinister look could well be the instrument of supernatural powers. Nowadays, however, it is more likely to be a much sought-after and rightly pampered pet.

Short-haired Cats

The Havana

The Havana is a dainty, fine-boned cat with a coat of rich chestnut-brown, showing no ghost points. The type is 'foreign' with wedge-shaped long head, large ears and a long tapering tail. The eyes should be almond-shaped and green in colour. The legs are slim with dainty oval paws and the foot pads pink. The colour is exactly the same as in chocolate-point Siamese and this cat would be better described as self-chocolate. The Havana's body is similar to that of Siamese but its rich brown coat is very different from that of the Burmese. Kittens are born with the coat colour they will carry through life.

The Rex

These cats, unlike any others, have curly or wavy fur. There are two kinds differing slightly in the shape of the head and thickness of fur. One is known as Cornish, and the other, Devon. Both have wedge-shaped heads and very large ears. The bodies are long with whip-like tails. They are both enchanting, looking, for all the world, as though they have just come out of the water with a permanent wave.

Cornish Rex

This is the original Rex mutation, first found in Cornwall in 1950. The early Rex was outcrossed to British short-hairs, but since 1965

Left: The beautiful Blue-Cream Long-hair.

breeders have aimed for 'foreign' type. The Cornish Rex resembles the sacred cat of Ancient Egypt. The coat forms waves over the body. The head, body, legs and tail are proportionately long.

Devon Rex

The second Rex mutation appeared in 1960. Matings to Cornish females produced straight-coated progeny, proving the two mutations to be dissimilar. This mutation was perpetuated by back-crossing the first filial generation to the sire. The Devon Rex coat is closely waved. Type is 'foreign', but the head is full-cheeked with a whisker break. Some folk find it hard to differentiate between the Cornish and Devon Rex. In fact, the Devon has a wider, pixieish face and the nose of the Cornish is more Roman. The Rex are endearing, mischievous little cats, very affectionate and playful.

The Korat

The Korat has been described as the cat with the heart-shaped face. It is a comparative newcomer to Britain, with a small head and big eyes which are a brilliant green. They are silver-blue in colour and look most gentle and appealing. They originate from Thailand and found their way to Britain via the USA.

The Manx Cat

The Manx differs from all other cats in that it has no tail and there should be a slight hollow where the tail should start. The head is round and large with a longish nose and full cheeks, the ears being a little pointed. The fur is short and soft and may be of any colour.

Because of their hoppity walk, they were once known as 'rabbit' cats. The litters may contain kittens without tails and with very short tails known as 'stumpies'.

It is not always easy to rear Manx kittens and very careful weaning is necessary. They are still bred on the Isle of Man where they first came from. Incidentally, the rump of the Manx is expected to be as round as an orange! Although when speaking of the Manx one generally thinks of the tail-less variety there are also show classifications for the stumpie and the tailed Manx.

The Abyssinian

First seen in Britain in 1869 and mainly originating in this country, this attractive variety is considered to be very near in outline to Ancient Egyptian cats. Murals and statues of the time illustrate cats of this shape. Type is 'foreign' with long body, head long and pointed, sharp ears and fairly long tapered tail. The Abyssinian differ from all other short-hairs in the unique coat of ruddy brown with black or brown tickings. There must be no bars or other markings. The chin should not be white, but it is difficult to breed out this defect. It is also possible to produce red and blue coated Abyssinians and these colours are recognized by the Abyssinian Cat Club.

The Russian Blue

This is a most beautiful cat, originally known as the Archangel Blue. The first imports were Lingpopo and Yula, both from Archangel (on

A red-coated Abyssinian.

the north-west USSR coast) and owned by a Mrs Carew-Cox of Saffron Walden, Essex, England. The breed is noted for its short, thick, silvery-blue coat of a seal skin texture and dainty build. Their heads are small, with green eyes and large vertical ears, and they are very silent, sweet-natured cats.

The Black Short-hair

A shining jet black coat with no white hairs or rustiness is not easy to produce, and a true Short-haired Black is most beautiful to see. Although once regarded as the 'familiar' of witches and connected with black magic, this variety with powerful body, deep chest, broad round head, and orange eyes is now a typical 'British' cat.

The White Short-hair
As in the long-hairs there are two varieties, one with blue and the other with orange eyes, i.e. Blue-eyed White and Orange-eyed White, the blue-eyed being affected sometimes by deafness. A very attractive cat, with pure white, short thick coat and no yellow tinges, the type as for other British cats. There is also a short-haired Odd-eyed White, with as in the long-haired variety, one eye orange and the other blue.

The Blue Short-hair, or 'British' Blue
A good blue is the most typical of the type required for the British short-hair varieties. It has a smooth, plush coat, powerful body, full broad chest and good round head with small eyes. The most popular of British, as opposed to foreign varieties. The coat may be light to medium blue but must be of an even shade throughout.

The Cream Short-hair
These are delightful cats with pale cream coats, good broad heads, small ears and big eyes which change from blue to copper colour. All kittens' eyes are blue when first opened and it is some weeks before the true colour shows. Creams are quite rare as it is not easy to breed them with no tabby markings.

The Silver Tabby, or Silver Short-hair
The pattern of markings should be as for other tabbies and the type is typically British. A most distinctive variety with background colour of pure silver and dense black markings. The eyes should be green or hazel.

The Red Tabby Short-hair
The same symmetrical pattern of tabby markings is required, but these should be a very deep red on a lighter red ground. The eyes should be hazel or orange. The concept that all red tabbies are male is incorrect, as from red and tortoiseshell breeding red females may be produced and a red male bred to a red female produces all-red litters of both sexes. There is also a brown tabby short-hair which is not so often seen. It has a typical British broad round head, small ears and big round eyes which may be orange, hazel or deep yellow, with its pattern of black markings standing out from the rich sable background fur.

The Tortoiseshell Short-hair
Coloured patches of black, red (dark and light) and cream, as brilliant as possible, make up the pattern of this variety with no white or brindling. Patching must be all over the body. They are female with the odd freak and sterile male cropping up occasionally. At least one of the parents must carry the colour gene for red.

The Tortoiseshell-and-white Short hair
These Torties are said to be very loving and maternal. The brilliant colour patches of black, cream and red should stand out clearly, but with additional areas of white. Colour patches should cover the top of the head, ears, back and tail, and also part of the sides. The white blaze on the forehead is light. Eyes should be copper or orange.

The 'natural' coloured Abyssinian. It is hard to breed out defects such as the white chin and the bars or other markings.

65

The Blue-Cream Short-hair

This is a rare variety in which the coat is intermingled pastel blue and cream and there is no patching. The type should be British. The cat is virtually a 'blue tortoiseshell' and invariably female. The variety may be bred through cream and blue matings.

The Foreign Lilac

This is as yet a rare breed in Britain, only having achieved Show Championship status in 1977. It has a Siamese-type body and its coat is of an elusive pink-toned frosty-grey with pinkish nose leather and pads. Because there are few cats of this type at this time, mating may be made with the Havana from which this type originated, but once more stud cats are available, doubtless one will see more of this attractive unusual cat.

Other comparatively rare breeds include the British Tipped, the Smoke Short-hair, the Bi-colour Short-hair and the Spotted Short-hair. The British Tipped, which is of British type with broad round head, small ears and short, straight broad nose, is different from other British varieties in that the undercoat should be white-tipped with any recognizable British colour, or tipped with brown, chocolate or lilac.

Oriental Spotted Tabby

Also a Siamese type, but has a different coat pattern – clear scarab (beetle) marking on head, unbroken lines running from eyes and pencilling on cheeks. This variety should have a short, fine glossy coat with thumb prints on ears, legs should be barred, spotted or both. It has a kinked tail.

The Foreign Black

Developed from crosses between the Havana and seal-point Siamese. The short, fine, jet black hair, should be minus white hairs or rusty tinge. Siamese type with long head, large ears and oriental green eyes.

The Foreign White Short-hair

The cat to surpass all other cats – that is how, naturally enough, the Foreign White Cat Fanciers' Association describe this variety. It represents a dream come true for its pioneer breeders who, more than sixteen years ago started work on the development of a pure white blue-eyed cat with Siamese body type and sound, lovable temperament. Today it is clear that the careful and selective breeding by those early breeders has brought success, for judges regularly comment on the wonderful temperament of Foreign Whites; and the beauty of the breed, with its shining, glossy white coat, long *svelte* Siamese lines and deep, deep sapphire blue eyes is apparent for all to see.

The breed was recognized for Championship breed status in June 1977. The first Champion was John Harrison's 'Scintilla Jou-Lin'. The first Premier was Eileen Scott's 'Alexa Jasper' and the first Grand Champion, Pat Turner's 'Scintilla Hsi-Ch'i'.

At the 1977 Supreme Show of the GCCF (five months after full breed status had been granted) Scintilla Hsi-Ch'i became Best

Left: Short-haired White kittens enjoy a romp in the sun.

Foreign Short-hair Kitten and finally Supreme Kitten. The following year the best Foreign Short-hair Kitten was again a Foreign White.

Not only are Foreign Whites successful at shows, they are also the most wonderful and lovable pets. In fact, ownership of a Foreign White is addictive, most owners deciding that two or more Foreign Whites must be better than one. For this reason kittens are usually in short supply and breeders with Siamese are often advised to mate their Siamese to a Foreign White stud rather than wait for a kitten from another breeder. Matings between Siamese and Foreign White produce 50 per cent Foreign White kittens.

Lists of Foreign White studs and kittens for sale are kept by the Foreign White Cat Fanciers' Association. This club was formed by the breeders who developed the breed and members are offered a complete service of meetings, advice, annual medal awards, trophies for wins at shows and participation in a specialist show run by the club.

The Burmese Cat

Burmese is a comparatively new breed to Cat Fanciers and came to Britain from the USA. The little brown cat from which the breed derives, 'Wong Mau', was taken to the USA from Rangoon, Burma, in 1933. She came into the hands of a Dr Thompson of San Francisco, USA, who was intrigued by the differences between Wong Mau and seal-point Siamese, the previously known breed of cat from the Far East, and in conjunction with a small group of geneticists and cat breeders carried out a programme of

The brown Burmese is an alert, affectionate and intelligent cat, always ready for a game. This variety is not a truly self-coloured cat; note how the colour shade darkens at the head, ears and tail.

Until 1955 most people thought of the Burmese cat as being brown. Today, however, there are several coat colours to choose from. This is a cream Burmese.

experimental breeding aimed at clarifying Wong Mau's genetical make up. This proved conclusively that she was in fact a hybrid of Siamese with another distinct breed which they called Burmese. The pure Burmese cats produced in the breeding programme had darker coats than Wong Mau, with less contrast in the coat colour between body and points and when these darker cats were mated together they bred true.

We are told that, like Siamese, these brown cats have been bred in Burma and other parts of the Far East for a very long time and were greatly valued, being the prerogative of the wealthy and of the temples. However true this may have been in the past it is hardly likely to be so now.

Brown Burmese (known as sable Burmese in the USA) are not truly self-coloured cats. Their coat colour shades slightly from a rich dark seal brown on the top of the back to a slightly lighter colour underneath and there is a slight intensification of colour of the points. The kittens when born are a *café au lait* colour which gradually darkens until they achieve full colour at nine to twenty-four months, depending on the particular cat. In these respects they differ from Havanas (the only other short-haired breed of brown cats) which are a uniform brown colour (redder in tone than Burmese brown) all over, the kittens being born the same colour as the adults.

The coat of a healthy Burmese is fine, silky, close lying and has a characteristic natural sheen. The cats are of medium size, strong and very muscular. Other distinctive features are the face (which is short, blunt wedge-shaped, with a short muzzle showing no jaw pinch), the ears (erect, wide at the base with the opening well to the front and with the top of the skull nicely rounded between the ears) and large, expressive eyes ranging in colour from chartreuse yellow to golden yellow. The tail is not whip-shape like Siamese and tapers only slightly to a rounded tip.

The cats are alert, active, intelligent and extremely friendly and affectionate, and it is undoubtedly these character traits which have been mainly responsible for their rapid growth in popularity. The kittens are most attractive in appearance, full of character and quite fascinating to watch.

Until 1955 most people thought of the Burmese as the brown cat and it is probably the brown Burmese with its beautiful eyes, which should be any shade of yellow from chartreuse to amber (golden yellow preferred), which is most popular. The Burmese cat does, however come in delightful colours of blue, chocolate, lilac, red, tortoiseshell, cream, blue cream, and chocolate and lilac tortoise-shell.

Unusual breeds of cats

There are a number of fascinating cat varieties which you may not be able to see in many places.

The African Wild Cat
The African Wild Cat comes from the open woodlands of Africa and south-east Asia. It has tabby markings, its basic colour ranging from grey to tawny yellow. It stands 35 cm (14 in) high at the shoulder, which is rather larger than most domestic cats. It appears that this variety was successfully tamed by the Ancient Egyptians, as its mummified remains have been found. Other small, wild cats, all of which are closely related, include the Black-footed Cat from South Africa, the Chinese Desert Cat, the Jungle Cat of southern Asia, the Sand Cat from North Africa and the Leopard Cat from western Asia.

American Short-hair
The American Short-hair has longer legs and nose than the British type; its muzzle is more square and its fur of harsher texture and of a wider colour range. Incidentally, the colour tortoiseshell-and-white is, in the USA, referred to as calico.

American Wire-hair
In 1966 a chance mutation produced a kitten with coarse, wiry hair in the litter of an American farmyard cat. By selective breeding this was introduced into American Short-hair types from which the breed differs only in coat texture.

Bombay Cat
This is an American breed. It is jet black and was produced by crossing American Short-hairs with the Burmese.

Cymric
This is a long-haired variety of Manx cat produced by chance mutations. It is tail-less.

European Wild Cat
Rarely seen these days, except perhaps in the Highlands of

Scotland. It has large, tabby markings and is distinguishable from the domestic cat by its larger skull and teeth and its tail which is rounded at the tip.

Egyptian Mau

Fascinating cats with tiger marking, bred artificially to resemble the cats of the Ancient Egyptians. The Americans recognize the breed in silver and bronze. In Britain, it has been developed from Siamese and has evolved of more foreign type, with a scarab-type (beetle-shaped) mark on the forehead.

Feral cat

Not altogether an unusual species, because it is a domestic cat, turned wild. Feral cats are distinguishable from the European Wild Cat by their pointed tail-tip and smaller head. Most domestic cats could fend for themselves if called upon to do so and, after several generations of living wild, would tend to revert to tabby coat patterns.

Japanese Bobtail

This is an ancient Japanese variety, unlike any other. Its tail is approximately 10–12 cm (4–5 in) in length, but is held curled so that it tends to look much shorter. Its back legs, which are long, are generally bent, which gives the back a level appearance. The Japanese Bobtail is tri-coloured, red, black and white, (some other colours are accepted in the USA). This cat is said to shed less of its hair than other varieties.

Maine Coon cat

Probably evolved through crossings between the short-haired cats of settlers and Angoras brought by sailors from the east. Requires less grooming than most long-hairs.

Peke-faced Persian

This is a breed of long-hair, recognized only in the USA, and developed from Red Self and Tabby Long-hairs with heavy jowls. It is unusual in that the nose resembles that of a Pekingese dog. However, as the breeding of this variety can lead to breathing problems and trouble with tear ducts (as indeed suffered by the Pekingese), there is some controversy as to whether this type should be perpetuated.

Ragdoll

This mutation developed in California from a Persian whose kittens, quite remarkably, seemed impervious to any form of danger, or pain. They are sensitive and extremely vulnerable cats, very loving and like the Birman in appearance.

Scottish Fold

This mutation has the disapproval of a number of feline authorities. It has drop ears and was developed from a kitten of this type born in Scotland. Think of a tabby with the ears of a British boxer dog – but in proportion to head size of course!

The Somali
The Somali is a recently developed mutation produced from long-hair kittens in Abyssinian litters.

The Sphynx
The Sphynx, recognized only in the USA and Canada, must surely be the equivalent in the cat world of Mexican hairless and Chinese Crested hairless dogs. It is a most regal animal, free of coat, except for a little pile, which feels just like velvet, on the face, and some hair on the testicles. Unlike hairless dogs, however, which have a high body temperature, the hairless cat does feel the cold. It is by no means unattractive to touch, or to look at.

Feeding, housing and care

Kitten care

Cats live for many years, so do not offer a home to one unless you are prepared to love and care for it all its days. Kittens, like babies, need plenty of sleep. They should have their own cardboard box, or basket, with a piece of blanket inside where they can sleep in peace, well away from draughts, and they should not be picked up too often. Nor should they be squeezed, for their bones are very soft and easily damaged. And never try to pick them up by the back of the neck; only their mother does this, when they are very tiny. Also, for both kittens, and cats it is most important to remove all bones from chicken and rabbit, as these sharp bones can cause great suffering and death by piercing the intestines, or catching in the throat.

The kitten's happy future
Cats are probably one of the most popular companions for the elderly, and have the added advantage that they are self-exercising – an important point for invalids or those with infirmities. In any case, the keeping of a pet often motivates the senior members of the community to go out to shop for food, thereby also encouraging them to eat, and to make provision for adequate heating at home, thus lessening the all-too-frequent risk of hypothermia.

For those who fear that they might pre-decease their pet, or are concerned that a stay in hospital would be an insoluble problem, charitable schemes are run in most areas of the country to deal with this problem. Speak to your vet if you have any fears, or a representative of the Cats' Protection League in your area. You'd be surprised how many people love cats!

Feeding

An adult cat needs two feeds daily, a light meal in the morning, and its main meal in the evening, which it may eat during the night. Don't fill the bowl with a day's food supply expecting the cat to come back to it. This will not only encourage flies, but discourage the cat who is a fastidious feeder and expects, and deserves, to receive his rations in a freshly washed bowl.

The cat is predominantly a flesh-eating animal whose diet should consist mainly of meat or boiled fish. Many cats prefer fish, which ideally should be boned. Not all cats share my own pet's liking for kipper heads and tails!

Meat can be given cooked, or raw, according to preference, but start as you mean to go on. The cat weaned on cooked meat may well turn his nose up when his dinner is served raw! Whatever you do, make sure that the meat is minced, or chopped into small pieces, as cats' teeth are designed for tearing rather than chewing; they also have a small mouth.

And if you don't want your cat to leave home, it's advisable to vary his menu. A weekly treat of lightly cooked liver or boiled rabbit will be appreciated; so will horse flesh, tripe and hearts. Some cats enjoy milky foods such as cereal and rice puddings and the occasional cat has a sweet tooth.

Always leave a fresh supply of water for your cat. Some enjoy a saucer of weak tea. My own Siamese is thoroughly spoilt and receives the cream from the top of the milk. If I don't bring the milk in before he gets to it I find the bottle top deftly hooked off and the cream sunk to a questionable level! There are cat owners who say that cats need only water, other who insist that a saucerful of milk be given each day. I should leave it up to the cat!

Cat lovers will do everything for their pets, but there is one thing many of them do not know and that is how to feed them correctly. A survey by the Pedigree Petfoods Education Centre recently showed that the majority of cat keepers hadn't a clue how much food they should give their pets, even if they knew what to feed them on. If you feed your cat on scraps from the dining table and the odd saucer of milk he may survive, but he certainly won't be getting the balanced diet that he needs to keep him in good health.

Nowadays a very large proportion of pet owners feed their pets on specially selected canned, or dry foods, which have been scientifically prepared to contain all the nutritional requirements of the animal, proving a boon to the busy owners who may not have much time to spend in the kitchen, but still want to do the very best for their cat.

You have the choice of giving a fully grown cat a handy sized can, roughly 182–189 g (6$\frac{1}{2}$–6$\frac{3}{4}$ oz) of a branded meaty product; half this portion again if he's a big cat and goes in for a lot of exertion. Or you can offer a meat and liver in gravy product, or a complete cat food containing energy food as well as meat, fish or liver. There are also convenient soft, moist cat foods which provide a balanced diet, and complete, 'dry' feeds which may be moistened with water, or milk, if the owner wishes. If you feed a complete, dry feed, do ensure that your cat has an ample supply of drinking water or milk.

By feeding good branded products you can be certain that your cat is getting all the minerals and vitamins – including the all-important thiamine – needed for perfect health.

These foods are better balanced and more complete diets than many human beings get. They not only meet your cat's nutritional requirements but have been tested to meet a cat's 'taste' in flavour and texture.

A question asked by many cat lovers is – can you give a cat bread

Left: Kittens need plenty of sleep. This Brown Tabby kitten has made herself comfortable in a hammock; but she should have access to a more secure bed too, e.g. a draught-free cardboard box or basket, lined with a blanket.

and vegetables as well as cat food? Yes, you can add a little bread or breakfast cereal to meaty products, but you don't really need to. And remember, a cat cannot take in a lot of starchy foods or roughage in the shape of green vegetables.

Water intake

While pet owners take great care over the feeding of their pets, they are possibly less conscientious about a pet's drinking needs. 'Should any water be given, together with the meal?' or, 'Doesn't my pet drink too much if it has free access to water?' are typical and frequent questions. They indicate a lack of knowledge not only on the amount of water needed, but also on the role of this key ingredient.

Fresh water should be available at all times to cats and dogs. They will not drink too much at any one time if they can drink whenever they wish.

Fussy cats

Cats are such fussy feeders that once they have developed a taste for one kind of food, they will sometimes almost starve rather than change. That is why it is probably best to feed them on a diet, scientifically prepared and tested specially for cats. But you will always find the awkward cusses who prefer to eat dog food. If it is a good quality food, it won't do puss any harm.

The fussiness of cats is sometimes encouraged, even started by their owners. If you feed a cat on nothing but fish or meat you must add milk every day, give sterilized bone meal for calcium, meat extract for thiamine, and a teaspoonful of cod liver oil once a week for vitamins A and D. So it certainly is simpler to wean your kitten on to a good branded product which contains all the essential cat nutrients.

Fat cats

Neutered cats sometimes get fat simply because they don't take so much exercise, and become lazy and lethargic. All cats are rather lazy animals, though they seldom get fat.

If you give your cat starchy foods such as bread and potatoes and similar types of table scraps, cut these out. You can also cut down the quantity of food you give, providing you make sure that the quality, nutritionally, is adequate for health.

You may be giving your cat too much milk, so try cutting this down, making sure the cat has enough to drink, of course, and harden your heart about those table scraps and titbits in between meals. If your cat seems unwell and overweight, do take him to the vet for a check up.

Housing

Nothing annoys the knowledgeable cat lover more than hearing a fellow-owner speak of putting the cat out at night; except, that is, hearing the fable that you never feed a farm cat, the idea being to keep it hungry, so that it will need to catch mice.

Right: "Can I have a bite?" Although cats can have bread mixed in with their meat, it must be remembered that it is not really necessary, and too much starch could make your cat fat.

It is strange how the idea of having to starve a 'mouser' persists. After all, in days gone by the farmer would not have expected a starving horse to pull the plough, and he himself would hardly expect to have to tackle a day's work out of doors, without sustenance. Good farmers consider the welfare of their machinery, but many have never thought seriously of the value of the farmer's friend, the farm cat.

The words 'Have you put the cat out?' are almost a music hall joke. One wishes they could be forgotten. Cats that are turned out at night are likely to be stolen, injured or killed. They may also get caught in traps or wander away and become strays. Worse, they could be picked up by some unscrupulous person whose aim is to sell cats to vivisection laboratories. Your cat is far too precious to be faced with such risks and, why after all, should he not share and enjoy the same fireside comfort as a dog companion? If introduced to the family dog from kittenhood, he is likely to want to share his pal's basket!

Ideally, the cat should have a soft, warm, draught-free bed. His cushion, covered in washable material, may be placed either in a basket raised from the floor on a footstool or box, or it may be in a large, lidless box, turned on its side and a narrow board fixed across the lower part of the front.

Cats are creatures of habit and if, in late evening, you let puss out and call him in again a few minutes later, perhaps by banging a spoon on a saucer, he will quickly develop a lifetime habit of coming in and settling down for the night. Investing in a cat flap is sound advice. Then your cat can rise and retire when it wishes. Also, unlike that inviting open window, it is not a temptation to burglars.

General care

Moving home

Several million families move to new homes every year, and though I do not subscribe to the view that cats care for their homes more than their owners, they do become very attached to their surroundings and finding themselves in an unknown place can prove a disturbing or alarming experience.

Cats, with that uncanny sixth sense of theirs, usually know that all is not as usual from the day that you first start your packing; they may even complicate matters, if given the chance, by disappearing for a few days as if trying to delay your careful plans, so try not to alter puss's routine, and keep him under close surveillance at this time.

On moving day, give puss a sedative, obtained beforehand from your veterinary surgeon, or your local People's Dispensary for Sick Animals. Place the cat in a basket, or other suitable container, with a soft rug in the bottom and sufficient ventilation, and put the basket in a quiet place, away from the noise and the bustle.

On arrival at the new house, again place the cat, still in its basket, in a quiet spot. When the bustle has died down, release the cat into a secure room, give it a meal and provide it with a sanitary tray. It should be kept indoors for a few days, being allowed to wander

Left: A cold, hard pavement is no place for a tired puss at night. Make up a bed for your cat in a warm place, and keep a litter tray next to it; or better still have a cat-flap fitted on the back door, so your cat can come and go as she wishes.

round the house, and become familiar with its new surroundings, and reassured that although it is in a different place, the people and household objects are the same.

There has long been an old wives' tale that, if you butter a cat's feet, it will settle in a new home; the theory being that, the fastidious cat, intent on licking its paws clean, will become oblivious to its surroundings. Try it, if you like!

What you should also do is purchase an elasticated cat collar. Some folk fear that, if the cat gets caught up in a branch, the wearing of a collar may cause strangulation, but the risk is negligible, for the elastic stretches sufficiently to free puss, or dislodge the collar itself. The benefit outweighs the danger, for an identification cylinder can be attached which unscrews to allow insertion of a slip with your name and telephone number – invaluable if puss should get lost or stray. The slip generally has a print-out of the words: 'Reward offered'. How do you value the return of a much loved puss? I always write the word: GENEROUS!

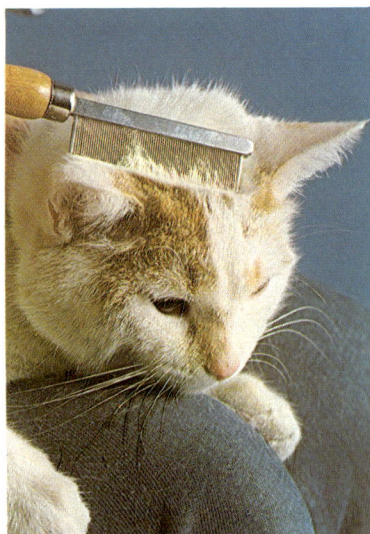

Above: If a cat's fur is not brushed regularly, the cat will lick down loose hairs when washing itself, which will form a fur ball in its stomach.

Grooming

A short time should be spent every day on brushing and combing. Although cats wash themselves regularly this is still necessary. Brushing will rid the fur of any loose hairs which the cat may lick down to form a mass inside, known as a fur ball. This could cause illness.

It is unwise to bath cats, except in extreme circumstances. Not only is the immersion resented, but the difficulty of drying thoroughly may lead to pneumonia.

Brushing will help to keep the fur clean and remove any fleas which the cat may have picked up. A cat should always be able to eat grass, which it may vomit together with any fur swallowed. If you haven't a garden, then grass should be grown in a pot or window box, for this purpose.

Holidays

One does come across folk who habitually take their pet with them for an annual holiday by the seaside, particularly if they stay in a caravan or holiday chalet. However, there is always the risk of puss getting lost, so it is safer to leave your pet at home where it can use its cat flap, and entrust a reliable neighbour with a key and feeding instructions. Or leave him at a well-run cattery.

What you mustn't do is leave an enormous quantity of opened food in the hope that this will last puss until you return. He will eat on the first day, then starve for the rest of your holiday.

There are excellent catteries in all parts of the country. The better they are, the more likely they are to be fully booked in summertime, so do make your cat's booking when you finalize your own holiday plans. Many catteries have outside runs adjoining each cat-house so that the cat may stroll out and enjoy the sun on a pleasant day. A proprietress I know even enlists the help of her family as 'strokers' so that the cats feel at home!

Right: The cat is a very clean animal and washes itself very thoroughly. But even this fastidious Siamese needs to be groomed by its owner.

What you will discover is that any cattery worth its salt will insist on seeing a certificate of inoculation against infectious enteritis. This is the most deadly of cat diseases and when it appears in a

Don't forget that arrangements must be made for your pet when you go on holiday. Ask a neighbour to come and feed your cat regularly and keep an eye on her, or better still leave her at a well-run cattery.

neighbourhood, it spreads so quickly, and so many cats die within a few days, that people start imagining that there has been malicious poisoning. Young cats, Persians and Siamese are particularly susceptible, and the disease is most common in summer. So have your cat inoculated well in advance of your holiday – it needs a booster every two years – and don't get uptight if you think that the kennel owner is being fussy. You wouldn't want your puss, or anyone else's, to die because of your negligence.

Very important, when planning your holiday, is to remember that you cannot take your cat out of Britain and bring it back again without puss facing six months quarantine in Ministry approved kennels. This is expensive for you and no fun for your cat either.

Neutering

Sadly, many thousands of unwanted cats and kittens have to be put down every year, because with the queen coming into season every three or four weeks in summer, there are just not enough homes to go round.

Luckily, much is being done to halt the birth of unwanted kittens by encouraging the neutering and spaying of cats not kept for breeding.

Neutering a tom cat is doing him a kindness, for undoctored he is a compulsive fighter, vulnerable to torn ears and other wounds and, in later years, as he finds himself in combat with younger partners, his injuries could be grave. After neutering, he loses the desire to fight, does not smell anti-social and prefers the comfort of his own fireside to a night on the tiles. The operation is such a simple one that it is possible to take tom to the surgery for neutering and bring him home with you a few minutes later.

Spaying a queen (female) cat entails a bigger, but routine operation, and a few days stay at the surgery. Between three and five months is the age recommended for the operation but, as in the case of the male cat, it can be done at almost any age. The fact that a female cat has had kittens is no deterrent.

Discipline and house-training

The cat is a naturally clean animal who, in adult life, tends to almost 'bust' rather than displease. If it makes a mess for any reason other than enforced confinement, don't delay in consulting your veterinary surgeon.

A kitten may be quickly house-trained by providing a litter-tray filled with sand, dry earth or, better still, specially prepared cat litter available from most pet shops and chemists. Put kitty on the

A cat sharpens its claws to keep them manageable and useful. Although your pet must be trained not to sharpen its claws on the furniture, it is up to you, the owner, to provide some kind of scratching post for this purpose. An old branch would do, or invest in a specially-made scratching post from a pet shop.

litter-tray after each meal and/or mistake and it will soon adopt the tray as its special toilet. But you must clean it out every day; otherwise, puss won't use it; and, when disinfecting, don't use carbolic, which is dangerous for cats. When puss is old enough to go out of doors the tray can be discarded. However, many flat dwellers have a litter-tray as a permanent fixture. You don't have to have a garden to keep a cat!

Your pet must be trained not to sharpen its claws on the furniture by shouting a loud 'NO' each time it starts to do so. If it is able to get into the garden it will most likely use a tree. If you are an apartment dweller, a scratching post may be bought from a pet shop.

Incidentally, you must never, ever, smack a cat – not to be confused with a playful pat in fun. Punishment of this type may cause the pet serious injury. And it won't serve your purpose. The cat will merely be resentful.

Pedigree or moggy

Most folk who have set their heart on buying a pedigree cat know exactly what they want, so that they may pursue the hobby of cat showing and/or breeding or merely cherish a specimen of what they believe to be the most beautiful variety of cat.

Many cat shows, however, have classes for pet cats which do not have pedigrees. These are not judged by a breed standard though they must be used to being handled by strangers and be in good health. Many children's cats, if well looked after, win prizes at shows.

Pedigree cats can, of course, command high prices, whereas it is possible to obtain a 'pet' cat in return for little or no charge by making a donation to an animal charity.

The oldest animal charity in Britain devoted solely to cats, is The Cats Protection League based in Horsham, West Sussex. This organization whose work is carried out through fifty branches in Britain, staffed by voluntary workers, rescues strays, unwanted, and sick cats, and rehabilitates, and rehomes them where possible. It informs the public on the care of cats and kittens and, because there are so many unwanted cats in their care, encourages the neutering of cats not required for breeding.

Left: There are almost always more non-pedigree kittens available than homes on offer. They make delightful pets and can be shown in special pet (non-pedigree) classes at pet shows. If you want to give a home to a cat, or kitten, contact the Cats Protection League.

Cat shows

At cat shows pedigree exhibits are judged by a 'standard', that is, one hundred marks are given to an imaginary cat that would be a perfect example of the variety.

These marks are given for the right shape of head, the ears, body and fur. The standard is agreed and approved by the Governing Council of the Cat Fancy, under whose auspices all recognized cat shows are held.

Few cats are perfect, but if one comes very close to the ideal and beats all other cats of the same colour in a class at a show, it may be awarded a challenge certificate.

A cat that wins three certificates, under three different judges, could become a Champion.

A cat may become a Grand Champion by winning three champion challenge certificates, at three shows, under different judges, but before entering a Grand Champion Class the exhibit must, of course, be a full Champion.

Neutered cats can be exhibited in neuter classes and become what is known as a Premier by winning at three shows under different judges, and a Grand Premier under the same rules and conditions as those for Grand Champion.

Judges examine every entry to assess the condition; also the head, the shape and colour of the eyes, the ears, body, tail and colour pattern of the fur where this applies.

All pedigree varieties for which an official standard has been approved by the Governing Council of the Cat Fancy, have an allotted breed number (*see* Chapter 3 – Schedule of breeds).

Breeders often try to develop cats of a new colouring and/or coat and type, a practice which has, in the past, resulted in large entries at cat shows of exhibits for which no 'standard' existed, such cats being registered as 13a: Any other colour (long-hairs); 26: Any other colour (short-hairs); and 32x for new colours of Siamese. Nowadays these new varieties are placed on an experimental register and given a provisional standard. Provisional recognition, and a breed number, may follow as quantity and quality increase, but championship status is only granted when one hundred breed members have been bred to standard. The cats, meanwhile, are entered in what are known as Assessment Classes, being judged not against other exhibits but on individual merit. The number of merit certificates awarded help towards the recognition of the breed.

The large orange (or copper) eyes of a Smoke Long-hair (Smokey Persian) make this beautiful cat almost irresistible. The show judges, however, will be less easy to win over. They will check that the colour of the coat hairs is the same right down to the roots, and that no white hairs are visible in the coat.

Types of shows and classes

The following are some of the abbreviations you will find in a cat show schedule:

L.H. – Long-haired; S.H. – Short-haired; A.V. – Any Variety; A.C. – Any colour; M. – Male; F. – Female; A. O. C. – Any other colour; A.O.V. – Any other variety; S.P. – Seal-point; B.P. – Blue-point; C.P. – Chocolate-point; L.P. – Lilac point; T.P. – Tabby-point; R.P. – Red-Point; GCCF – Governing Council of the Cat Fancy.

Numerous cat shows are held throughout the year, ranging from the friendly exemption show, an ideal launching pad for the novice exhibitor, to the sanction show, usually staged by a breed club or society who have not yet tackled the pinnacle, the organization of a championship show. However, all these events are held under the auspices of the GCCF and run according to their strict rules. Challenge certificates can only be awarded at Championship

Shows, the best known of which is the National Cat Club Show, which one might be forgiven for referring to as the Cat Lovers' 'Crufts'!

There are often classes, even at Championship Shows, for non-pedigree exhibits. These give youngsters a chance to proudly show off their pets, and family moggies are groomed until they gleam. There is not a 'standard' for non-pedigree exhibits. They are judged on beauty of appearance and general condition; also on temperament, so an appealing cat with a tangled coat and spiteful nature would stand little chance of gaining an award.

There are many enthusiastic exhibitors among the non-pedigree

This tabby tom cat might stand a chance in the non-pedigree exhibits at the cat show, in spite of his bitten ears from alley fights.

fraternity and the holding of such classes for much-loved household moggies does much to foster pet owner education and care.

Cat shows are advertised in the newspaper, *Fur and Feather*. The GCCF publish a list and, of course, membership of breed and other cat clubs ensures receipt of advance information.

Buying the show cat

How do you buy, or breed, a potential show winner? You might as well ask: 'How long is a piece of string?' However, you will stand the best chance if you visit a recommended breeder and buy a kitten from proven winning stock. At the time of purchase you should receive a certificate of pedigree and you can, for a small fee, transfer registration of ownership into your name with the GCCF.

Many reputable breeders advertise kittens in *Fur and Feather*. You can locate the cat variety you wish through a breed club or, as previously suggested, by speaking to exhibitors at a show.

If it is your intention to show your kitten, say so; otherwise, you could end up with a charming, healthy kitten, which will make a decorative household pet but falls far below the show standard which you, the novice, cannot be expected to recognize.

The show

If you see a show advertised and would like to enter your cat, note the address of the show secretary and write for a schedule/entry form, remembering to enclose a stamped addressed envelope.

The schedule will list the classes to be held and you must check in the Definition of Classes those for which your pet is eligible; for instance, a novice class is open to exhibits that have not won a first prize under GCCF Rules, a limit class to those that have not won more than four first prizes and so on. And there are special classes for kittens, adolescents and juniors.

Having sent off your completed entry form and fee you may eventually receive an entry, or tally number. Or you may not receive this until you arrive at the show. Don't panic if an envelope fails to arrive, or hesitate to contact the secretary if you have any problems. Organizers are used to helping newcomers sort out any troubles, and to giving useful advice.

You, or your representative, must accompany the cat, placed in a suitable container, to the show. And be prepared for puss to be veterinarily examined before admission is granted.

Exhibits must have clean ears and their coats must be free from pests. No queen may be exhibited within two calendar months from the date of kittening. No exhibit that has been de-clawed will be accepted. The vets are within their right to ban any animal they consider unfit. Obviously this is a rule that is in all owners' interests.

There are special classes for kittens, adolescents and juniors at cat shows, so these Red Tabby Long-haired kittens might well be in with a chance. However, their owner must remember that Long-haired cats need grooming every day and particularly thoroughly before a show.

You must take to the show some food for your cat, a drinking and a sanitary tray and, of course, a clean blanket for it to lie on which MUST, like all the other items, be WHITE. None of this equipment must bear any distinguishing marks and blankets must be plain woven. A pretty coloured blanket to tone with pussy's marking would be of no help at all. Judges are instructed to pass by any cat that is distinguishable in any manner by its equipment.

If you have visited a dog show you will have seen the exhibitors parading their dogs in the ring, much credit being due to the handler. It is debatable indeed whether some dogs would reach such dizzy heights were it not for the skill of the person on the end of the lead.

The cat owner, on the other hand, must rely on the presentation of the exhibit and the grooming it has received, for exhibitors are not allowed near the pen while judging takes place and may even be asked to leave the room. Award slips are later affixed on a board and award cards placed on the winning cats' pens.

One of the things which cannot fail to impress the layman visiting a cat show, is the high standard of hygiene that is usually apparent. Exhibitors are advised to wipe the bars of the pen with a mild non-toxic disinfectant, and the judge, after handling each and every cat, dips his or her hands in a similar solution.

Cat shows not only offer the opportunity for friendly rivalry but provide a pleasant day out for exhibitors and visitors alike. There are usually stalls where one may purchase cat foods and accessories, as well as little knick-knacks, and there are breed club stands.

Judging and stewarding

How is the judge qualified to decide the best of exhibits which to you appear to have equal merit? Judging usually stems from years of successful cat breeding and the respect and acclaim of the breed clubs. Certainly it is not possible to become a judge overnight, or without years of stewarding, learning to make the task of the judge very much easier.

It is the steward's job to see that the disinfectant spray on the judge's trolley is full, that his Judge's Book is written up, before his arrival, with the numbers of the classes and exhibits to be judged, and that when each class is at an end, the judge signs the tear-off slips signifying the winners, which the steward then takes to the secretary's table. A steward should be knowledgeable, but at times unobtrusive, unfailingly helpful, and extraordinarily efficient. Most of them are!

A tortie sunning himself in a summer meadow.

Index